THE A
OF
T E AENEI

Current and forthcoming titles in the Bristol Classical Paperbacks series:

THE ART
OF
THE AENEID

William S. Anderson

First published in 1969 by Prentice-Hall, Inc.
This edition first published 1989, by arrangement with Prentice-Hall, Inc., by
Bristol Classical Press
an imprint of
Gerald Duckworth & Co. Ltd
61 Frith Street
London W1D 3JL
e-mail: inquiries@duckworth-publishers.co.uk
Website: www.ducknet.co.uk

Reprinted 1994, 2000

A catalogue record for this book is available
from the British Library

ISBN 1-85399-131-7

Printed in Great Britain by
Booksprint

❧ CONTENTS ❧

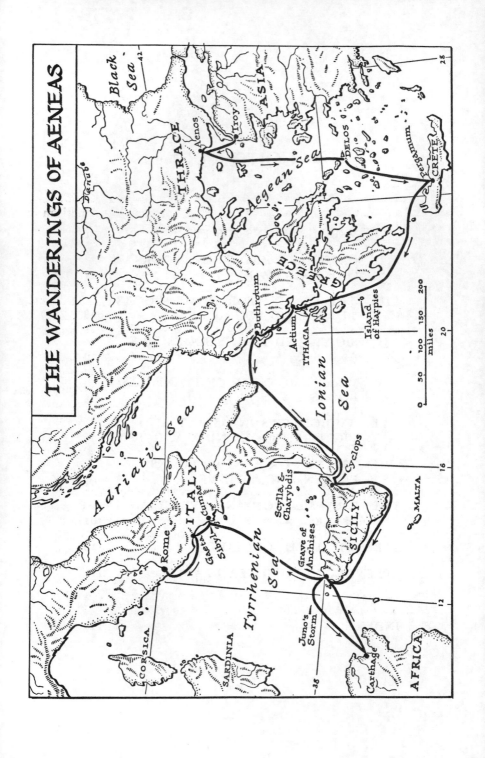

THE WANDERINGS OF AENEAS

Black Sea

Danube

ASIA

THRACE

Aenos

Troy

Aegean Sea

DELOS

Pergamum

CRETE

GREECE

Buthrotum

Actium

ITHACA

Island of Harpies

Ionian Sea

miles
0   50   100   150   200

Adriatic Sea

ITALY

Rome

Gaeta
Cumae
Sibyl

Tiber

Scylla & Charybdis

Cyclops

Grave of Anchises

SICILY

MALTA

Tyrrhenian Sea

CORSICA

SARDINIA

Juno's Storm

Carthage

AFRICA

28

20

16

12

38

42

⋅⋅§ PREFACE §⋅⋅

This book was written in Rome during the academic year of 1967-8, while I was serving as Professor-in-Charge of a program for American college students, which was designed to bring back to life for them the city of ancient Rome and the Roman world that they were studying in the United States. In writing it, I was myself inspired by my great affection for Rome, Classical, Medieval, Renaissance, and Modern, and by my sense of what in Vergil's *Aeneid* might most usefully be emphasized in the late 1960's. Working with the students in the Inter-collegiate Center for Classical Studies, poised near the summit of the Janiculan Hill, proved a pleasant and informative way of ascertaining the aspects of Vergil that merited emphasis.

By 1967, there were, I think, four main areas where Vergilian scholars focused their attention, each of them considerably influenced by historical and critical developments since the end of the War in 1946. They were: (1) Vergil's use of his literary heritage, Greek and Roman, especially of Homer. The emphasis was now on creative inno-vation rather than on mere borrowing or imitation. (2) Vergil's use of imagery and symbolism. Starting from the achievements of New Criti-cism, scholars such as Poeschl and Knox had paved the way for exciting new readings. (3) The structure of the Vergilian hexameter, of individual episodes, books, and finally of the entire epic. Both Duck-worth and Otis devoted much attention to various structural concerns. (4) The problematic interpretation of Aeneas within the epic and in relation to Augustus, the figure in contemporary Rome to whom he obviously alluded. Here, the jaundiced attitude toward any concen-trated political power, which Hitler had earlier inspired, had been focused, by the genius of Syme, on Augustus in his *Roman Revolution* (1939), and events of the Post-War period seemed only to confirm doubts about the once-hailed Golden Age in which and for which Vergil supposedly wrote. Was the *Aeneid,* then, an exaltation of the achievements of Augustus who, like Aeneas, brought peace and a new political order to Italy and the world; or was it a pessimistic revelation of the inhuman costs of that New Order, which robbed Augustus of his essential humanity and rapidly turned the principate into the troubled reigns of his Julio-Claudian successors? I tried to discuss each of these issues in the book and point the way toward answers.

In the twenty years since the publication of this book, as is evident from the bibliography, there has been no abatement of interest in the *Aeneid* and its absorbing critical problems. On the whole, though, exclusive preoccupation with either structure or symbolism has declined, as though for the time the achievements of the period up to 1970 were significant enough to require a period of quiet assessment. But the Post-War developments in literary theory have brought a renewed interest in Vergil's use of his literary tradition, as the intricacies of "intertextuality" or "contextuality" have been probed. And the problem of Aeneas continues to provoke readers and scholars. Against the more extreme and even the moderate views, that Vergil raises serious questions, through Aeneas' abandonment of Dido and killing of Turnus, about the methods and goals of Augustan autocracy, it is possible to discern today, in 1989, a conservative trend that emphasizes once again Vergil's positive view of Aeneas and therefore of Augustus' regime.

In 1981-2, Classical scholars celebrated the 2000th anniversary of Vergil's death. In the outpouring of articles and books that marked the occasion, it was clear that the *Aeneid* remained the focus of burning interest. I believe that that remains so today. Thus, on the mere twentieth anniversary of the publication of my book, I am delighted to have it re-published, with the hope that it will stimulate readers to discover the infinite riches of Vergil's inimitable epic.

Berkeley, California, 1989

Corrigendum: **Magus** for *Mago* on p. 84, line 7.

◈ I ◈

VERGIL BEGINS HIS EPIC

Vergil occupies a central position in the history of epic. On one side of him towers Homer, on the other Dante and other Renaissance epic poets until Milton. Whereas Homer mastered the art of oral composition and produced the most sophisticated poetry ever achieved in that challenging medium, Vergil lived in an era that knew only written or literary composition and had long utilized writing to examine, analyze, and defy the archaic principles of Homeric epic. The Age of Heroes had long ended when Homer attempted to capture their significance; by Vergil's day, Greece and Rome had experienced so much more history that the very concept of the hero was a near absurdity. For nearly a century, as a result of political troubles emanating from the Roman Forum, the Mediterranean world had been increasingly convulsed, and especially since Caesar had crossed the Rubicon, turmoil had prevailed. Vergil's contemporaries tended to flee from epic as a genre devoid of vitality, preferring such forms as elegy, lyric, drama, and satire. Or if they did attempt epic, they either adopted a mythological theme, such as the ever-successful story of Jason and the Golden Fleece, or they prostituted themselves to the ambitions of a politician and devised a "heroic" account of some military exploit or other.[1] In spite of the apparent obsolescence of epic and the disappearance of the heroic mentality, Vergil wrote the *Aeneid,* a work which is not only the greatest piece of Latin literature, but also the poem which endowed epic with a new vitality—so that it could survive until Florence and Dante produced another ideal combination which could begin a new epic under the guiding influence of Vergil.

Today, when we read an epic, we are dealing with a "dead" form. The word "epic" still possesses some power, especially for the advertisers of historical novels and the historical extravaganzas of Hollywood, but epic poetry no longer attracts poets, no longer is written. To read an epic like the *Aeneid,* then, is to grapple with

1

unfamiliar poetic conventions, a strange culture, and a complicated historical background: those are the immediate difficulties. But reading the *Aeneid* also leads to the discovery of a hero viewed with a penetrating and almost frightening understanding that makes him, despite his Roman armor, a man that we could easily recognize today. It is the purpose of this volume to assist the modern reader of the *Aeneid* to find underneath the dead form the living poetry of Vergil.

The first conventional element of an epic was the prologue; in the *Aeneid*, the prologue consists of the first thirty-three lines. Since the beginning of any work requires the utmost skill from a writer, a close reading of Vergil's prologue may help us grasp some of his basic methods and so facilitate our understanding of later portions of the *Aeneid*. I shall analyze the prologue in convenient units, each presenting an important aspect of Vergil's art.

I

I am the man who once worked out my song on the slender reed-pipe; then, I left the woods and compelled the neighboring fields to obey the farmer, no matter how greedy he might be, in a poem that pleased the cultivators of the fields. Now, however, it is the horrible arms of Mars and the man which are my theme . . .

In the late fourth century, long after Vergil's death and the gradual disintegration of Roman civilization, the industrious amateur scholar Servius compiled a huge commentary on the *Aeneid*. Servius found information which he chose to believe, and he solemnly reported that Vergil began his epic not with the now famous words *arma virumque* ("arms and the man"), but with the four lines translated above. No reputable scholar today accepts Servius' word, preferring to believe that these lines were composed by some admirer to appear under a portrait-bust or picture of the dead poet. However, these lines are relevant to our interests for two reasons: they show what a poet would *not* insert in his prologue, or anywhere in a proper epic poem, and they report authentic details about Vergil's earlier poetic career.

An epic poet could not begin his poem with an autobiographical statement or discuss elsewhere his earlier poetry, because tradition had established—and would maintain firmly until Dante's epic—

the convention that epic poetry was *impersonal*. This tradition of impersonality, beginning with Homeric epic and continued by later writers, sprang from several related sources. In the first place, no poet can honestly say that a poem is all his, created and finished by his conscious intelligence at every point. As poets have told us long before the Romantic era and many times since, poetry of the proportions of epic or drama is never fully explicable as a personal achievement. Therefore, the epic poet does not call attention to himself as he begins his narrative; instead, he invokes a Muse, the symbol of the inexplicable element in his marvelous creation. In the second place, the material of epic forces upon the poet an impersonal stance, for he stands removed from it by centuries.[2] Homer felt this distance with particular force, since his tenuous link with the past was oral traditions, and so he appealed to the Muse as the authentic source of historical fact. She was the daughter of Memory; she knew better than he what had really happened. Vergil, who undoubtedly realized better than Homer how little historical fact resided in his epic, nevertheless affected to be writing of events more than a thousand years earlier, over which he could claim no real control. So he too donned the mask of impersonality. What the audience expected to hear—and what he certainly wrote—was a brief account of the matter of the poem, along with an invocation of the Muse; it was the poem, not the poet that counted.

The impersonal stance of the epic poet is not something to which he reluctantly assents, as though, apart from the useless constraint of convention, he would immediately release his egoism. On the contrary, epic, like drama, gains from the seeming impersonality or objectivity of the poet. In epic the narrative progresses without obvious interventions of the poet, seeming to have a life of its own that, in the best poems, resembles life as we know it at the deepest level. Aeneas suffers at Troy what anyone who has lived in our own war-torn world can easily imagine; Aeneas does cruel things to Dido and Turnus which we all know are done all the time from necessity or from false arguments of necessity. The fact that Vergil offers no patent verdict on such events, but lets them impinge upon the reader with full potential ambiguity, shows how much can be done with this epic impersonality. It is the poetic responsibility of the epic poet—and his opportunity—to shape his narrative so that his audience experiences and judges the events for itself. In the varying judgments on the *Aeneid* and its major characters we see evidence of Vergil's faithfulness to tradition and successful exploita-

tion of the opportunity. Elsewhere we shall note how a certain sub-
jectivity merges with this pose of impersonality; now let us turn
to Vergil's earlier poetic career.

Born in 70 B.C., the year that Pompey first became consul, Vergil
grew up in an Italy that first dreaded, and later suffered the civil
war that launched Caesar against Pompey, then Caesar's heir Oc-
tavian against a series of rivals, including at last Antony. Young
Vergil apparently came to Rome in the troubled 50's in order to
learn law and the art of public speaking; apparently, too, he found
the environment intolerable and fled to the Bay of Naples and the
comforting retirement of an Epicurean society. From forensic art
he turned to poetry. Shortly after Caesar's murder (44 B.C.), he pub-
lished his *Eclogues,* pastoral poems whose fictitional stance assumed
a shepherd playing on his pipe.[3] Some of these poems, as one might
expect, express the poet's aversion to the present political chaos—
always through an invented speaker—but most of them are non-
political. They talk of an ideal pastoral world, not quite Arcadian
nor Sicilian nor Italian, where goats and sheep may freely graze
and their herdsmen may look forward to happy love and success
in their musical contests. This lovely set of poems won the poet im-
mediate fame.

Vergil's next work, a much more substantial poem, took him
seven years to produce, and by the time the *Georgics* appeared
(30 B.C.), Octavian had defeated his last and most serious foes,
Antony and Cleopatra, and was ready, as Augustus, to begin his
long reign of relative peace and reconstruction.[4] It was with the
vision of this eventual peace that Vergil devised, during the many
years of agricultural decline, his poem on the importance and
moral value of farming. Unlike the writer of the lines above, he
would hardly have claimed that he indeed successfully compelled
the fields to yield to farmers; his theme, that men should perceive
the importance of farming, hardly touched the farmers, but im-
pressed the urban moralists and some gentlemen-farmers (from 30
B.C. to the present). Nevertheless, the artistry is evident, and the
positive tone and the penetrating poetic vision of a farmer's sig-
nificance show how far he has left behind his largely negative Epi-
cureanism. The farmer's intelligent, often violent struggle against
adversity in order to raise his animals and crops—what Vergil at
one point calls his "cruel toil" (*labor improbus*)—anticipates the
heroic and compromised efforts of Aeneas.

In 30 B.C. the times seemed right for a positive epic about Rome,
now that the long period of civil war had ended and the immediate

future under the young, energetic Octavian promised much. And Vergil himself, at forty, had grown enough in artistic capacity and poetic vision to dare this demanding task. For the remaining eleven years of his short life, until his premature death in 19 B.C., Vergil worked at the poem. That last year, still not entirely satisfied with it, he decided to retire for three years to Greece and devote the entire period to meticulous revision. Once he reached Athens, however, he changed his mind; he started back to Italy, but the fever he had picked up in Greece grew worse, and shortly after the ship landed at Brundisium, late in September, he died. The poem was not finished. In fact, Vergil felt so unhappy about publishing the *Aeneid* in its incomplete condition that he called for the sheets of manuscript, as he lay dying, in order to burn them up. Fortunately his friends refused to grant that last wish. Two of them, able poets themselves, were commissioned by Augustus to edit the work. Exactly what their editorial efforts amounted to is not entirely certain. Later commentators like Servius and Donatus report theories of earlier scholars which modern students of the *Aeneid* still accept in general, namely, that the two editors worked with the greatest fidelity to Vergil's text. They may have eliminated some unfinished passages or lines, but not many, for they left a large number of incomplete hexameters in each book, including one at 3.340 which is incomplete in sense. It is in this context that Servius tells us that the four lines cited above, which had been written by Vergil and placed at the beginning of the epic, were removed. Scholars do not accept this statement, as I mentioned above: it seems incredible that an editor had better taste than Vergil or knew the poetic conventions of impersonality more exactly. Vergil began his poem conventionally and powerfully with the words which we shall now consider: *arma virumque.*

II

Arms and the man I sing

The two epics of Homer, which determined subsequent epic conventions, began as follows: "Anger sing, goddess, the anger which possessed Peleus' son Achilles" (*Iliad*), "The man describe to me, Muse, the versatile person who wandered far" (*Odyssey*). I have deliberately translated the Greek in a way to preserve the original word order, for it is important to see that the epic poet began with a noun which introduced the main subject of his poem immediately. Although any audience would inevitably react to the artistic techniques employed in epic, although oral and literary poets obviously must devote great care and skill to the means by which they narrate events, nevertheless all that was taken for granted in the tacit agreement between poet and audience, and he began by satisfying curiosity about the story. Homer drew a sharp distinction in his two openings between the two heroes and the way he chose to emphasize them; and Vergil, keenly aware of his predecessor's genius, adapts what he can of the two different emphases. In the *Iliad* Homer focused attention on the anger of Achilles, not on Achilles the total hero; for the inhuman passion negated the hero, brought ruin upon the Greek army, and finally crushed Achilles beneath an unbearable personal tragedy. In the *Odyssey*, on the other hand, Homer presented the man Odysseus in all his versatility; the integrated man, achieved after long years of misery before the epic begins, wins his return home and then recovers family and political status as he richly deserves. Homer illustrates two of the principal emphases in Classical heroic epic: the poet could pursue an essentially tragic vision and describe the passion which conquers the man, or he could work out a hopeful picture of life by creating a hero stronger than his passions and the sufferings imposed upon him from without.

After stating the main theme of the poem in a single noun, Homer used verbs referring to the poetic narrative process: "sing," "describe." Both of these verbs, we note, are imperatives. Imbued as he was with a feeling of the impersonality and irrationality of poetic composition, Homer instinctively avoided the personal and instead appealed or prayed to the Muse to perform the narrative *through* him. It might be argued that Homer's "prayer" is so perfunctory as to be nothing more than a vestige, even in his day, of what once was a meaningful invocation. Certainly Homer expected to and did do a great deal of work on his own for the success of his epics. Even so, he respected the convention that minimized his personal achievements, that regarded the cooperation of the Muse as a close second in importance to the interest of the audience.

Vergil alters the Homeric pattern in two significant ways: he uses a double-noun construction to account for his theme and he dismisses the appeal to the Muse until line eight, meanwhile emphasizing his own personal achievement as the poet ("*I* sing"). The choice of two nouns to define the material of the epic has often been explained as simply an attempt to remind the reader of the *Aeneid* that the one poem of twelve books would vie with the twenty-four books of the *Iliad* (with its concentration on warfare) and the twenty-four books of the *Odyssey* (with its concentration on a man). Vergil was inevitably vying with Homer; he was attempting to write for Rome an epic that would summarize the genius of the nation and the modern spirit, just as Homer so well captured the spirit of Greece at the end of the eighth century B.C. Much important work has been done in recent years to demonstrate the artistry of Vergil's competition with Homer.[5] There is one constructive pattern which most ancient readers detected; modern readers can also benefit by following it. During the first half of the *Aeneid*, Vergil takes his hero through a series of wanderings and modernized temptations which aptly parallel many of Odysseus' experiences before he reached home; during the second half, Aeneas goes through a war which Vergil deliberately compares with the Trojan War, and event after event finds its prototype in the *Iliad*.

The early Vergilian critics, who swarmed over his epic almost as soon as it was published, seem to have spent much of their efforts vainly attempting to elucidate Vergil's relation to Homer. For some, eager to depreciate the Roman before the Greek, Vergil could be dismissed as nothing more than an awkward plagiarist. Others felt the originality of Vergil and recognized the general principle of *creative imitation,* but they lacked the language to explain adequately their positive evaluation of the Roman achievement. More often than not, they could only point to an imitation and assert, without adequate critical argument, that it was better than Homer. Throughout this study I shall comment on the fruitful way in which Vergil utilizes Homer—we are no longer interested in saying who was "better" or "worse"—but I should like to suggest here some features of his creative imitation. When we compare Aeneas to Odysseus, we immediately recognize important differences. Vergil deliberately referred to the known heroic stature of Odysseus in order to bring out the special qualities of his hero and his hero's experiences. Odysseus sails from victory at Troy, Aeneas from utter defeat. Odysseus heads for wife and home, and for every delay is culpable and receives eventual punishment; Aeneas loses wife and home but learns from a vague series of prophecies that a new wife and home await him in a distant land, all so vaguely put that his delays and half-hearted commitment to his destiny win our sympathy. Odysseus enjoys Circe and Calypso and honorably flatters Nausicaa, then goes home to rejoin Penelope with little express embarrassment; Aeneas, a widower, falls in love with Dido, but his love leads to disaster for himself and suicide for Dido, a symbolic victim of the ruthless Roman quest for national greatness. Similarly, when we deal with the second half of the *Aeneid* and consider its use of the *Iliad,* we should be able to perceive how sharply the Italian war differs from the Trojan. Perhaps the most intriguing problem which Vergil presents us is to decide which of his characters parallel which of Homer. Is Aeneas Paris, Hector, Agamemnon, Menelaus, or Achilles? What about Turnus? Is he another Menelaus, as he claims to be? The fact is, of course, that the parallels are inexact; Vergil uses the Homeric prototype here, as earlier, to bring out the un-Homeric aspects of his personages.

It is not enough, however, to describe Vergil's opening as a skillful allusion to inevitable rivalry with Homer. To be sure, he used two nouns of different orders, one referring to a person, one to a thing, and the nouns suggest main elements of the two Homeric narratives. Two nouns together, however, interact; they cannot be absorbed separately as mere equivalents to separate Greek epics. When George Bernard Shaw entitled his comedy *Arms and the Man,* he knew exactly what he was doing and exactly what Vergil meant with his pair of nouns: they affect each other. Shaw humorously explores some of the paradoxical ways in which warfare affects the personality of the warrior. One appreciates the comedy all the more if he has read the *Aeneid* and grasped the near-tragic vision which Vergil presents of Aeneas the man of arms. Homer knew that warfare can turn a man into a beast, but in the *Iliad* war remains a fact with which men must deal; within the limited context of battle, men can become heroes. It is part of Achilles' tragedy that he can no longer accept the war as a necessary fact for himself. Vergil goes beyond Homer, since he does not present war as a necessary or desirable fact, and furthermore he shows not only that war brutalizes men, but also that men alter the meaning of war. Note, however, that he does not define Aeneas from the beginning as a tragic warrior, as Homer does Achilles. Instead of the negative term "anger" (later elaborated for its ruinous effects), Vergil uses the neutral word "arms," which he explains in the next lines as crucially important for the establishment of Rome. Together, "arms and the man" could be viewed as positive words, interacting creatively to make possible the good that undoubtedly existed in Rome. So from the beginning Vergil has started a theme of rich ambiguity, a theme which runs through the poem and remains provocatively rich even after the last lines.

This Vergilian theme of arms and man is so crucial that the reader should be prepared for it a little more elaborately. Vergil narrates two distinct occasions of war: the fall of Troy and the conquest of Latium. In the first, Aeneas meets defeat; he battles heroically—and his triumphs are not neglected—but the gods do not permit him to die, with conventional heroism, fighting for Trojan home and country. Although briefly bestialized by the exigencies of desperate resistance to the Greeks, Aeneas remains uncompromised; and it is evident that the gods have selected him because he has more importance as man than mere warrior. The second war is more complex. It starts under checkered circumstances, not without some responsibility on the Trojan side. It continues despite many cruel losses on both sides. Aeneas loses control of his passions and slaughters indiscriminately until at last he vents his anger on the guiltless Lausus and the guilty, but devoted, father Mezentius. Neither of these victories is clean and glorious, neither entirely tarnished by circumstances, but our uncertainty as to the attitude to adopt toward them applies to Aeneas as well. What is this war doing to him and to his ultimate goal? We see now that Vergil never intended to limit our sight to arms and Aeneas in themselves. We are always concerned, as we were but rarely in the *Iliad,* with the ultimate purpose to which this warfare is instrumental. Aeneas, while being a man, also stands for Rome itself. If his victories are compromised, what happens to the Rome he founds? That is the tragic question which Vergil makes us face in Book Twelve, as we watch the encounter between Aeneas and Turnus. Without any obvious guilt on his part (such as Achilles' anger), Aeneas becomes so involved in the Italian war as to render his final victory equivocal.

A few words about Vergil's verb "I sing." Just as Vergil felt free to exploit Homeric convention and to present a theme of complexity that accorded with the new complexities of civilization seven centuries after Homer, so he altered somewhat his relation to material and reader. I have already emphasized the tradition of *impersonality* and insisted that Vergil could not have begun with a set of autobiographical lines. Now it is time to note the other facet of the poem: with all its impersonal narrative devices, it is also highly personal. A recent writer has used the term "subjective," and perhaps that is more serviceable here, to avoid the awkwardness of the pair "impersonal" and "personal." [6] Vergil's subjectivity is developed from a post-Homeric attitude in Greek and Roman writers, who openly placed themselves in their poetry, expressing attitudes toward narrated events and openly influencing readers. It is too much to detect in "I sing" an assertion of this artistic method. The reader, however, will do well to notice how often and ambiguously Vergil suggests attitudes, especially sympathy for Aeneas' victims.

III

I sing of the man who was the first to come from the shores of Troy, an exile according to destiny, to Italy and the shores named after Lavinia. (1–3)

Just as Aeneas provides the connecting link between Vergil's adaptations of *Odyssey* and *Iliad*, functioning as both Odysseus and the hero of the *Iliad*, so Aeneas permits the development of another crucial theme of the Aeneid: the movement from Troy to Italy. Aeneas leaves his defeated and ravaged city of Troy and makes his way across the Aegean through other parts of the Mediterranean toward his ultimate goal of Italy. In Italy he fights to win a home for himself and his people, and victory brings a dynastic marriage with Lavinia, daughter of the king Latinus, who rules in the neighborhood of Rome (the name obviously suggesting the Latin peoples who eventually would align themselves with the future of Rome). This transition from defeat in the East to victory in the West is so important to Vergil that we should spend a little time now alerting the reader to its symbolic possibilities in the *Aeneid*.

In the myths about Troy, there is little doubt that the city deserved its destruction. A heritage of deceit and ruthless exploitation culminated in the selfish lust of Paris, who stole Helen, the wife of the man who was his host in Sparta, and heedlessly took her back to Troy, where the Trojan leaders permitted him to enjoy his criminal passion. Homer adds to this heritage of evil by staging a violation of truce negotiations: Pandarus shoots Menelaus, the injured husband, at the moment when a carefully arranged duel has promised to settle the war with a minimum of bloodshed. Thus, although the individual Trojan might feel deeply the defeat of his country, it was conventional to depict the end of Troy as an event favored and promoted by gods as well as men. To escape from Troy, defeated but alive, would mean to leave behind the sinful taint of the past and to seek some new, creative future. And since Aeneas was permitted to escape, it should also follow that he himself was hardly tainted by the misdeeds of Paris and other members of Priam's family. In Italy, destiny had chosen a new environment for the Trojans under Aeneas; there, the good aspects of the Trojan heritage could flourish, stimulated by the change of milieu and the proximity to the new Italian culture.

At one level, then, the flight from Troy to Rome signifies the abandonment of a corrupt past and dedication to a creative future in a new land—all this happening far back in the mythical past just after the Trojan War, that is, around 1200 B.C. But Vergil saw more immediate, contemporary relevance in the Trojan theme, and he shared his insight with other writers of the period. Also writing in the 20's, Horace published a poem in which he made much of the Trojan War, the move to Italy, and the hostility of Juno (which we shall consider in the next section). Horace's theme concerns the absolute and necessary break between guilty Troy, which must remain ruined and uninhabited, and the new land founded by the Trojan survivors. To this extent, his short Ode 3.3 parallels Vergil's epic. Horace also links this remote mythical past with the present by comparing the reward of apotheosis won by Romulus, Aeneas' descendant who founded Rome, with the divinity to be granted Augustus for his heroic achievements. For Horace the myth of Troy-Rome was a symbolic story which could be applied fruitfully to contemporary history. Vergil made a similar application on a larger epic canvass.

The unforgettable condition of the first century B.C., before Augustus decisively altered the trend of events, was civil war. If war is evil, civil war is evil compounded many times; and the Romans easily viewed their civil war in terms of an archetypal myth, such as that of Troy. Their ruthless leaders had brought ruin on the state, in which the Senate and the people had shamelessly or weakly connived, and the result was a war which ravaged Italy and the empire and consumed the flower of the population. Octavian (soon to be honored with the title of Augustus) closed that century of enmities and bloodshed when he defeated Antony at Actium in 31 B.C. Thereafter, he dedicated himself to restoration, winning the confidence of most people during the 20's, so that it indeed seemed as though a new era had opened—as in fact it had. That transition from civil war to the Augustan Age of peace and prosperity could easily be interpreted in the myth's terms as a progress from corrupt, defeated Troy to new, hopeful Italy. As we shall observe, Vergil reminds us more than once of the likeness between Aeneas and Augustus. He constructs his epic so that the move from Troy to Italy can be interpreted on two levels: on that of Aeneas' experience and on that of contemporary Rome of the 20's B.C. The literal story gains from the symbolic possibilities.

At the level of Aeneas' experience, fate and exile have poignant significance. The flight from Troy goes counter to Aeneas' personal desires, for his attachment to his native land makes of him a reluctant, unhappy leader who regrets every foot that separates him further from Troy. If he had had his way, he would have died in the futile defense against the Greeks. Barring that, he would have attempted to rebuild Troy from its charred foundations after the departure of the Greeks. When that was prevented, he actually tried to settle as close to Troy as he could, either disregarding divine advice or twisting it to fit his own preconceptions. What compelled him to go into "exile" and made that exile permanent was fate. Fate, which had decided to make Troy into Rome, chose unhappy Aeneas as its instrument. During the whole period of several years —as many as seven according to one reckoning—when Aeneas was guiding the Trojan survivors toward Italy, he himself felt like a mere exile, torn from his homeland and forced to go elsewhere, but unable to commit himself to any place but Troy. He constantly looked *back* to Troy, not *forward* to Italy and the future. Only when he reached Italy and glimpsed, with the help of a supernatural vision, the potential results of his efforts in the new land did Aeneas cease to regard himself as an exile from Troy and start to think eagerly of settling in Italy. He had at last effected the transition in himself from Troy to Italy, from defeat to victory, from ruinous war to creative peace; and that personal transition represents the change produced in Vergil's Rome by what he would choose to call the force of fate.

IV

Much he was tossed on land and sea through
the violence of the gods who acted on behalf
of savage Juno's memory-stimulated anger;
much he also suffered in war. (3–5)

Although Fate rescued Aeneas from the ruins of Troy and guided him to his eventual victory and new home in Italy, the passage was not tranquil. In addition to the fact that Aeneas had to overcome his own reluctance and uncertainty, he found himself in direct opposition to the will of vindictive Juno. This imperious wife of Jupiter, the most powerful goddess of the pantheon, had many reasons for hating Aeneas and his destiny, some of them connected with old memories involving Troy, some related to the future of

Aeneas' settlement; all these will be explained in line twelve ff. Juno, in fact, serves as the principal force of complication in events seen on the divine level. What Fate and Jupiter will, she opposes. Since Fate can never ultimately be halted, Juno's resistance is vain, but it brings with it much trouble for all the human beings involved. She works against Aeneas both through other gods— Aeolus in Book One, Allecto in Book Seven, and Juturna in Book Twelve—and through the major mortal foes of Aeneas—Dido of Carthage and Turnus of Ardea.

Vergil makes of Juno a vivid dramatic character, but he exploits her so significantly that we can profitably schematize her role and thereby attain considerable insight into the basic polarities of the epic.[7] Juno is represented as a proud and angry woman who vents her wrath on innocent mortals as harshly as she can. Although she pits herself, on the divine level, ostensibly against Aeneas' mother Venus, her most important enemies are Fate and Jupiter, who, as "father of gods and men," acts synonymously with Fate. Jupiter exhibits few dramatic characteristics: he is calm, confident, and triumphant in the end. So she represents the forces of Disorder in the *Aeneid,* he the ordering forces. On her side Vergil places anger and other passions, irrational thinking and action, destructivity of others and self—Dido commits suicide finally—and such symbolic occurrences as storms on land and sea, fire, war. On Jupiter's side we find serenity, creative action, above all the building of Rome. There is inevitably a certain pallor about Jupiter's side by comparison with Juno's, and this extends equally to Aeneas, the human being chosen by Fate and Jupiter to carry out the dispassionate creative work on earth. Against him are arrayed a series of exciting people whose emotions are hot and easily win our sympathy, as Vergil clearly intends them to: Dido, who ruins herself and her new city for irrational, but all too genuine, love; Turnus, who ruins himself and much of Italy for a combination of love and ambition, which he pursues egoistically long after they have lost their justification. Dido, with her distracting passion, and Turnus, with his war perverted into a personal vendetta, are both extensions of the ruinous, futile, grudge-cherishing anger of Juno.

Many scholars have criticized Vergil for making Aeneas less vivid than Dido and Turnus; many readers have felt that Aeneas comes off badly at Carthage and that his killing of Turnus in the closing lines of the epic hurts him in our eyes. We can also say that Juno is far more interesting than Jupiter or impersonal fate. To answer the objection exhaustively at this stage is unwise, but I shall sketch out some lines of reply which the reader can bear in mind as he becomes acquainted with the epic. On the one hand, good things and good people are simply less exciting than bad things and people. Consider such antitheses as good king vs. bad, judge vs. criminal, good woman vs. "bad," angels vs. devils, trusted civil servant vs. unscrupulous politician. There are far more enthusiastic readers of Dante's *Purgatorio* than of *Paradiso* from the same epic. Again, people do not become dispassionate and "saintlike" without a struggle. As the *Confessions* reveal, Saint Augustine knew from personal experience most of the sins which he later so eloquently condemned. And Aeneas himself, so bland superficially, is a turmoil of emotions inside. Here we should note the passive verb-forms with which Vergil has rendered Aeneas' experiences in these three lines: he *was* tossed, he endured. In what sense can we dismiss the hero as a "passive" character; to what extent must we grasp the fact that his "passivity" is the necessary price he personally must pay, the behavior required by Fate for true creative Order?

The word "passive" carries a tinge of contempt in English; it suggests that someone has let himself be imposed upon and so not acted "like a man," not even felt any manly reactions. But there is an ambiguity: some people are passive because they have no spark of life to them, others because, after long internal struggles, reason prevails over emotion and commands acceptance. The second kind of "passivity" can be heroic. In a sense it is a Vergilian adaptation of the qualities residing in Homer's "long-suffering Odysseus." [8] Odysseus, too, was tossed about on land and sea; in fact, Homer refers to such experience in the prologue to the *Odyssey*. Such suffering taught Odysseus enough so that he had his quick temper and vigorous intelligence well under control when finally he arrived back in Ithaca. Without that special ability to endure, to remain passive, he could never have avenged the crimes done by the suitors and regained his power. All this is superbly dramatized when Homer has Odysseus, transformed into a beggar, slink into his own palace and appeal for food from the men who are stealing that food from him, usurping his home, and even attempting to seduce his wife.

This grand concept of a "passive" hero could not simply be appropriated by Vergil; it required considerable modification. The times for which the *Odyssey* was composed enabled Homer to create a hero who is primarily an individualist, the ideal man in conflict with forces, both human and divine, natural and supernatural, which would negate his being. Although Odysseus has responsibilities to his crew and his wife, they do not dominate his personality, and Homer explicitly exculpates him in his prologue for failing to bring his crew safely back to Ithaca from Troy. Vergil's age could not tolerate a primitive individualist; it would have been inconceivable to disregard the guilt of a leader who returned alone without his men. Thus Aeneas never has freedom of action. Every act of his is conditioned by the presence of his people, his son, and by the *public,* not private, destiny marked out for him. Aeneas' passivity is not, like Odysseus', partly a device, a temporary role from which he can eventually emerge to take violent, passionate vengeance on his enemies. Aeneas gets no personal satisfaction except to realize that through his efforts others will benefit, for he must permanently crush his strong feelings, subordinating them to the demands of public service. It is only necessary to compare Odysseus and Aeneas as they suffer storm and shipwreck—the opening incident of the *Aeneid*—or as they react to the women they encounter en route to their destination—Circe, Calypso, and Nausicaa vs. Dido—to see what Vergil has done to develop the theme of the self-denying public servant.

Passivity does not come to Aeneas in a moment. Vergil chooses incidents carefully and constructs his epic to illustrate the slow acquisition of the requisite "heroic" qualities. In Book One, after several years of adjustment to exile, Aeneas has already advanced toward passivity. His personal account of the fall of Troy in Book Two reveals what a strong, impetuous warrior he once had been, how powerfully he resented the loss of his homeland. Even though he had left much of that impetuosity behind, he plunged violently into his affair with Dido, ignoring his duties until sharply recalled to them. Then, with great reluctance, he obeyed. Not until he finally arrived at Cumae and was granted a vision of the future did he commit himself fully to his public role. Thereafter, his dedication is unquestionable; he does consistently what is demanded of him, though not without feeling deeply the cruelty of his position. More than once he cries out against the war into which he has unwillingly been plunged—particularly against the deaths of dear comrades like young Pallas, but also against the losses that he will be compelled to inflict personally upon the enemy. That hesitant moment at the end, before he drives his sword into the heart of Turnus, is but the last of a series of poignant moments when the individual Aeneas, a man of deep humanity, protests against, then accepts "passively," his public responsibility. Poet that he is, Vergil does not prejudice our attitude and make us feel that we are reading some Sunday school story about a typically uncomplicated, simple-minded saint. There are losses as well as gains in the character and achievement of Aeneas as a direct consequence of his passive behavior. As the Odyssean individualist he is completely destroyed by his responsibility; even much of his humanity must yield to political exigency. All this makes the Rome he founds a much realer entity, and Vergil is even prepared for us to raise the question: Was it worth it, to subject a man's character to that end?

V

His sufferings were directed toward the goal
of founding a city and bringing gods to Latium,
from which would result the Latin nation, the
leaders of Alba Longa, and finally the walls of
lofty Rome.   (5-7)

Odysseus, as I noted above, had one principal goal: to get himself home alive. Aeneas' goal involves him in the fates of his fellow Trojans, who have chosen him as their leader, and in the course of history; with the result that his sufferings, referred to that distant end, allow him little option. His national significance dwarfs his personal desires. The city which he founds is Lavinium; Vergil alludes to it in line two. But it is significant that the founding occurs outside the epic; Vergil does not even dramatize the scene of partly personal satisfaction when Aeneas, peace achieved, finally does establish the city which, unlike the many false starts registered in Book Three, will win divine favor. Lavinium represents the union between Lavinia and Aeneas, Latin peoples and Trojan survivors, and so Vergil refers to it by the phrase "Latin nation" (though the phrase has additional possibilities). After some thirty years, however, Aeneas' son will transfer his power to a stronger position in the Alban Hills, called Alba Longa. Then, three hundred years later, Romulus and Remus, royal princes of Alba involved in dynastic struggles, found Rome, Rome that will swallow up Alba Longa, the rest of Italy, and ultimately control most of Europe, the Near East and North Africa.

It was long after Vergil, indeed years after Dante, that historians began to suspect that history had no overriding "pattern." Greco-Roman writers, historians and poets alike, confidently perceived patterns in events or, to put it another way, forced events into a preconceived pattern of human, not historical construction. When Vergil began work on the *Aeneid* he had many different facts and patterns to choose from. To use some of the details of lines five to seven as examples, there were divergences among the sources available to Vergil on the ancestry of Romulus and Remus and on the chronology of affairs. The founding of Alba could also be assigned to several different people. In almost every instance, Vergil thought through the stories and made a poetic selection among them, in order to secure a uniform thematic sequence. Scholars do find occasional inconsistencies—which may indicate some change of intention on the poet's part—but probably they arise more often from ordinary human error. In 1.267 ff., a sketch of the future informs us that Aeneas' son Ascanius (the son brought from Troy) will transfer the seat of power from Lavinium to Alba. In 6.760 ff., on the other hand, another prediction declares that Aeneas' son Silvius (born in Italy after marriage with Lavinia) will found Alba. In any case, these "errors" are so few and the grasp of detail so strong that Vergil is ranked by most critics as one of the greatest scholar-poets of all time. This was indeed what his period most valued in a poet: *doctrina* (learning) that could be put to the use of his *ars* (native talent).

In this prologue, Vergil presents the historical pattern with restraint, for he recognizes the danger he incurs by combining the story of a man and the history of the Roman people. Had he desired to produce a mere historical allegory, the task would have been easy; and had he chosen to view Aeneas as a nonhistorical variant of Jason or Odysseus, that, too, would have reduced his problems. It is the delicate combination of the two elements, historical and legendary epic, that tests his genius. There are strategic points where the unfolding of the historical pattern seems necessary and valid, but these are remarkably few, always subordinate to the narrative of Aeneas' direct experiences. Only after he has shown Aeneas in action during the storm of 1.81 ff., both against the cosmic opposition of Juno and nature and against the human discouragement of his men and himself, does Vergil interrupt the narrative to direct our attention to the ultimate goal of all this suffering. The pattern, set forth by Jupiter in 1.257 ff., extends beyond the founding of Rome, through the magnificent achievements of the early Roman Republic, down to the revival of Roman integrity in the peace founded by Augustus. As part of the pattern Jupiter schematizes the three foundings—of Lavinium, Alba, and Rome—to form a magic number 333. There is no note of danger or menace in the future; it seems one continuous development of empire. Whereas this prediction was not given to Aeneas in Book One, but to us the audience, in Book Six Aeneas himself eagerly hears the future. The moment is carefully chosen. Having just completed his long journey from Troy, Aeneas has at last arrived at the sacred site of Cumae near modern Naples, a place that early established links with Rome. It is, so to speak, the ideal moment for him to glimpse his future, as he first sets foot in the promised land. Vergil, therefore, creates a potent situation, not without ambiguity, for Aeneas' vision of the future comes while he is visiting his dead father in the Elysian fields; it might be only a "dream." Clearly, it is represented as something less than certainty. Yet Aeneas does commit himself enthusiastically to that uncertain future, and thereby the crucial break between Trojan and Italian-Roman Aeneas is accomplished. From this point Aeneas looks forward, not backward to dead Troy.

Once more, at the end of Book Eight, Vergil finds a poetically valid opportunity for outlining the future. This time it is in the context of the war that Aeneas has had forced upon him by Turnus. Not having planned to conquer his new land by force, Aeneas was obliged to secure allies where he could and to find a complete new set of armor. The allies come from the little village where Rome one day will rise and, in much greater numbers, from the Etruscans somewhat to the north; the armor for the new war in new, untainted circumstances is provided by Vulcan, husband of Aeneas' mother Venus. On the shield Vulcan has worked out in careful arrangement important relevant events of Roman history. Within a band depicting in separate panels a series of military trials from Romulus' day to Catiline's conspiracy in 63 B.C., Vulcan has produced a colossal central scene about Actium and the final achievement, through war, of genuine, creative peace. To the audience the significance of all this is crystal clear: the war of Aeneas in Italy, with its brief positive results (the Trojan settlement and the founding of Lavinium), anticipates the titanic events of Vergil's contemporaries, when Augustus closed a century of civil war. It is important for Vergil, however, not to overstress Aeneas' personal identification with or understanding of these future deeds. In the miraculous environment of the Elysian fields it might be possible to penetrate the future; back on earth, Aeneas can only take a simple, uncomprehending pleasure in the pictures he sees. Ignorant of events, *ignarus rerum* (8.730), "he shoulders the glory and destiny of his descendants," as Vergil suggestively puts it.

Probably the most telling proof of Vergil's skillful juggling of Aeneas' personal experiences and of Roman historical patterns can be seen in the way the epic closes. With but few exceptions, every line of Book Twelve refers patently to the circumstances affecting the forces of Aeneas and Turnus and their leaders; the references to Roman customs and future history remain implicit, a second, subordinate level of meaning. When Aeneas kills Turnus, Vergil stops. When Vergil stops, however, critics begin to raise their voices, many of them attempting to rewrite the conclusion for poor Vergil, who, if not judged incompetent by some egregious commentator, is usually dismissed with the assertion that premature death prevented him from finishing the epic properly. We shall have to deal more fully with the Aeneid's last lines when we treat the last book. There I shall operate from the assumption that they do represent Vergil's intentions for the epic's conclusion. Hence it is highly significant that the poet focused on Aeneas at the close and did not obscure the clarity of the picture by explicit references to the future. A lesser poet might have brought Aeneas back triumphantly to Latinus and then staged a marriage or peace ceremony which would be allowed to allude to the Augustan future. Vergil does not, and the poetic significance of the conclusion is thereby freed from restrictions. We are, I think, meant to wonder about Aeneas, as he holds that bloody sword which has just eliminated Turnus, and if this leads us to doubts and hesitations about the Augustan achievement too, well and good. In any case, the victory over Turnus produces an ambiguity that affects Aeneas directly. Vergil did not intend to hang the story of Aeneas upon the heroized story of Augustus; he meant to view Aeneas as a Roman, with sufferings and stresses that might anticipate those of later political leaders—including of course Augustus—in general, not specific terms. Aeneas is not simply Augustus. To put it another way, the poetic pattern achieved by Vergil's sensitive imagination dominates any historical patterns that he could have adopted from others.

VI

Muse, tell me the reasons. In what aspect of
her divinity was Juno injured and why was she
so aroused that she, queen of the gods, forced
a man noted for *pietas* to experience so many
changes, to face so many trials? Is it con-
ceivable that so much anger resides in the hearts
of gods? (8–11)

It is often said that "divine machinery" constitutes a standard portion of epic. Thus, in the middle of the first century A.D., Lucan consciously broke tradition when he created an historical epic on a recent subject (the wars between Caesar and the followers of Pompey) and removed gods and goddesses entirely from the scene. He obviously regarded gods as a disposable element of epic, but we should be careful of the phrase "divine machinery." Although many epics were composed in Greece and Rome in which the gods could be dismissed as mere mechanical devices not strictly relevant to the essential poetic theme, the best epics integrate gods with action and themes—some more than others—so that "machinery" does not accurately describe their function and significance. Homer illustrates the integration of the gods with the story on a loose basis in the *Iliad,* in much tighter terms in the *Odyssey.* Even in the *Iliad,* where the gods often behave childishly—now with total indifference to men, now with naked prejudices—there are moments when Zeus and the others provide a moral perspective on the war and Achilles' behavior which the human heroes cannot supply. Thus, all the trouble of the Greeks was due first to the impiety of Agamemnon, then to his outrageous arrogance toward Achilles; both times, he incurred punishment from the gods. It is in the *Odyssey,* however, that the gods function most economically in support of morality. From the opening scene we learn that Zeus upholds moral behavior and punishes immoral acts. The remainder of the epic follows from this beginning: Odysseus' crew and the suitors in Ithaca suffer destruction for their immoral folly, whereas Odysseus, Penelope, and Telemachus are reunited in Ithaca because of their common moral awareness. Besides Zeus, who represents this neat moral order, only two deities play significant parts in the *Odyssey*: Poseidon and Athena. The first does much to hurt Odysseus, from the day the hero blinds Polyphemus (son of Poseidon) until the moment, many years later, when Odysseus lands in Ithaca. Athena, on the other hand, acts as a counterforce to restore her favorite to his home. It is plain that Poseidon harasses Odysseus with some justice, for the circumstances surrounding the injury to Polyphemus raise questions about the hero's moral awareness. When, however, he has been punished by shipwreck and hopeless isolation in the middle of Poseidon's realm, the sea, Odysseus comes to his senses slowly, wins the favor of the goddess of wisdom Athena, and with her help secures his return. His arrival in Ithaca marks the end of Poseidon's power over him, that is, the end of his moral culpability. From that point, he is the man of ethical intelligence, specially assisted by Athena, who sets about ordering his home.

One could argue that the treatment of the gods in Homer illustrates two quite distinct stages in the Greeks' development toward moral sophistication. It is also legitimate to point out what Vergil probably saw in the two poems: namely, two aspects of the gods as grasped by the genius of Homer already in the eighth century B.C. On the one hand, the universe seems to have little or no moral order, the gods ignore human misery, and men grope alone through tragedy and death for ethical insight. This is the world of Achilles and warfare. On the other hand, the good seem often to prevail while the evil perish, as if there were an overriding moral order that asserts itself: this is the world of the *Odyssey*. What Vergil does, at any rate, is to refine the moral insights of Homeric epic and use the gods to clarify the ethical order of his Roman epic. It is beside the point to ask whether Vergil believed in his Juno, Aeolus, Venus, and Allecto and then to dismiss the gods of the *Aeneid* as mere "divine machinery" because we cannot imagine that he did. I personally feel that Vergil penetrates closer to the moral core of the universe than any ancient epic poet, perhaps any ancient poet at all; and the respect which later Christians showed toward his work suggests that they perceived the same religious-moral depth.

Vergil does something which Homeric epic never achieved: first, he creates a division among the gods between forces of Order and Disorder; and secondly, he presents in Aeneas a hero whose most signal quality is *pietas,* yet who, in spite of that, becomes the innocent victim of Juno, Aeolus, Allecto, and all the human incarnations of Disorder. Aeneas has not blinded a Polyphemus or done anything equivalent to merit the anger of Juno; nor, when the war starts in Italy, does he fall victim to the selfish passion that undermined the heroic stature of Achilles. Aeneas exhibits a new kind of tragic heroism: that of the public servant who labors for others selflessly, suffering deeply the unmerited attacks of those who, for various reasons, resist his efforts.

It is important to grasp the meanings of the Roman word *pietas* inasmuch as this, the only quality assigned Aeneas in the prologue, furnishes the most common description of him throughout the epic: *pius Aeneas.*[9] The adjective and noun describe the right relationship that exists between a human being and (1) the gods, (2) his public responsibilities as citizen or political leader, (3) his family, and (4) other human beings. Long before Vergil, tradition had assigned to Aeneas remarkable family devotion. The story was told that at the time of the fall of Troy, Aeneas, who had somehow won the favor of the victorious Greeks, was given his choice of what he would carry out from Troy for himself. When he chose to rescue his father rather than take a vast amount of gold, the admiring Greeks awarded him an epithet that caught some of the aspects of Latin *pius*. We can see how much Vergil has enlarged the significance of the episode in order to expand the application of Aeneas' *pietas*. To have Aeneas make a deal with the Greeks would not do, for that smacks of treason. Therefore, Vergil's hero fights to the bitter end, fully responsible toward his beloved Troy, and he acquiesces in the departure only under repeated divine pressure. The pageant of that exit from Troy is a masterpiece of Vergilian symbolism. Not content with the simple legend that Aeneas carried his father from the defeated city, Vergil adds to the picture little Ascanius stepping along at Aeneas' side, and in the father's hands he places a small receptacle containing the penates or household gods. Aeneas, in the center of the tableau, fulfills the first three aspects of *pietas*. Not only is he obeying the gods, but he is carrying the religious symbols which will serve as the basis of important rituals in his new land. Not only is he showing family devotion with his filial act toward Anchises his father (as legend prescribed), but he is leading his son by the hand so as to continue the family. Creusa, his wife, loses her way in the confusion and, through no fault of Aeneas, but passionately regretted by him, disappears. The total family group centered on Aeneas represents the public mission of the hero, who serves as the necessary link between old Troy (Anchises) and new Troy in Italy (Ascanius). Aeneas' duty, which he selflessly carries out, is to bring the Trojans to Italy and make possible their lasting settlement. This he admirably accomplishes, then dies three years later without having had time to enjoy his achievement.

The poignant theme which Vergil raises by his question about divine anger lies at the heart of the *Aeneid*. Why does Juno so angrily oppose Aeneas when, at first sight, he seems to represent something unqualifiedly good, *pietas* incarnate? Surely, we must feel as we read the prologue, the gods are making a mockery of human virtue. But our initial reaction becomes refined as we see the complex elements involved in Aeneas' destiny, for Vergil intends us to feel the tension between the creative functions represented by *pius Aeneas* at his best and the destructive acts to which he seems forced by that same *pietas*. Juno, who hates Troy and Aeneas, loves Carthage and Dido and certainly feels considerable affection for primitive Italy—that is part of the significance of her epithet *Saturnia* for Vergil—and its proud leader Turnus. Aeneas, too, starts to love Dido and settle in Carthage, but his duty to gods, Troy, and Ascanius compels him to abandon the queen and so bring about her despairing suicide. When he enters Italy he does his best to make peaceful arrangements, but war is forced upon him, and later the arrangement for a duel between the two leaders that would spare further bloodshed is treacherously broken by the enemy. However, the moment comes when again Aeneas' duties, above all to a fallen ally, drive him to slay wounded Turnus after a moment's hesitation. It is significant, I am sure, that before the death of Turnus Vergil has paused over the reconciliation of Juno, who at last accepts the founding of Trojan Rome and retires tranquilly, even happily from the scene of conflict. At the end we know that Aeneas has performed his duty toward gods, country, and family. Now the terrible question raises itself in a new manner: Is it possible for so much anger to exist in the hearts of *men?* Must the final act of Aeneas' achievement be one in which one facet of *pietas* negates another; must he angrily kill Turnus to satisfy his regret for young Pallas, with the result that he ignores his humanitarian instincts for a noble foe who has openly confessed defeat? That, at any rate, is the way Vergil has concluded his epic. It is toward that ambiguous answer (or new question?) that the opening question proceeds.

After introducing some of his central themes in the first eleven lines of the prologue, Vergil effects his transition to the first main episode involving Aeneas (34 ff.) by a passage which accounts for the hostility of Juno to the Trojans. I shall deal with it briefly in the next chapter. It is time now to trace the development of these Vergilian themes and to discuss some of the techniques Vergil perfected to narrate his great story. For that purpose, we turn to Books One and Two.

❧ II ❧

CARTHAGE AND TROY: BOOKS
ONE AND TWO

The first major event of the *Aeneid* is the storm which batters
Aeneas' fleet as it leaves Western Sicily, driving it far off course
southward on to the coast of Carthage. Aeneas had sailed happily,
with every expectation of being on the last leg of his long voyage
from Troy to his promised land. But Juno, angrily watching him,
seized her opportunity. Her irrational fury erupts in the storm,
which Vergil presents in a symbolic concatenation that is funda-
mental to the entire *Aeneid*. A masterful study of this episode by
Victor Pöschl nearly twenty years ago revolutionized interpretation
of the epic.[1]

Unlike Homer, Vergil wrote in a tradition of dense literary sym-
bolism, and he is the Latin poet who most perfectly realizes the
possibilities of such techniques. In the storm episode, symbolism is
built up from the metaphors describing the fury of Juno—wounds,
fire, pain; the personifying terms for the winds of Aeolus—furious,
destructive wild beasts or unruly subjects; and finally elaborated in
the representation of the tempest itself, with the result that Vergil
quickly establishes for us in a powerful dramatic scene the thematic
terms for Disorder. The ordered pattern of Aeneas' ships, extended
out over a calm Mediterranean, is shattered by Aeolus' winds, just
as Aeolus' orderly kingship is convulsed by his unwise decision to
release the winds. But Vergil does not leave us without countersym-
bols for Order. Although Aeneas is helpless at this stage—signifi-
cantly so—Juno's irrationality and Aeolus' unkinglike acts do not
prevail. Neptune, king of the waters, rises to calm the storm and
rescue the fleet from danger. At sight of the disturbance the god's
first instinct is anger, but, unlike Juno, he controls himself, and
this self-control constitutes the prerequisite for rational, creative
action. The winds are "routed," Aeolus soundly rebuked, and, with
the loss of a single ship, Aeneas reaches safety. He has seven ships
with him at landfall; twelve others have been driven apart from
him, but not to destruction as he first fears.

24

The climactic development of this opening symbolism occurs in the simile which describes Neptune's pacifying acts and ends the whole episode. The first simile of the epic, Vergil has attached it carefully to the symbolism of Order, and it repays study (1.148 ff.). Using anachronism with skill, Vergil evokes a scene of the Roman civil wars—potentially recognizable to every adult in his first audiences. Just as an unruly mob, assembled for some destructive purpose, was occasionally restored to sane quiet by a respected statesman and gave up the weapons which fury had furnished, so Neptune, himself controlled, controls the unruly winds. Thus Vergil has extended the range of this first episode into the political sphere; we are to see how the storm suggests war in general, the civil wars in particular. Neptune's activity, on the other hand, indicates the goal of peace and political stability toward which Aeneas is groping, then beyond that, points to the achievement of Augustus, who, like Neptune and the statesman of the simile, quieted the storm at sea and the mob at Rome. The simile establishes the polar significance of two terms: *furor*, the madness of the mob, seen also in the winds and Juno; *pietas*, the virtue by which the statesman prevails and Aeneas will prevail. In the apocalyptic vision that Jupiter will soon give Venus and us, it is no surprise to discover that Augustus' achievement is represented allegorically as the effective imprisonment of *Furor impius* (1.295). The very incarnation of disorder will at last be overcome.

When the seven ships make land, Aeneas demonstrates his leadership. Leaving the crews to light fires and prepare exhaustedly the few supplies they have, he climbs a cliff to scan the sea for the other ships. Nothing appears. Still refusing to yield to weariness or discouragement, he locates a herd of deer, kills seven, and brings back the rich meat to his men. Then, as they eat the unexpected banquet and share wine which he has brought from Sicily, he heartens them further by a speech in which he urges them to look to the future, remembering all that they have already survived.

It would not be hard to show that most of these actions and words have their parallels in the *Odyssey*. And Vergil does expect his reader to interpret Aeneas in the light of Odysseus. But he does two things here to extend the significance of this passage: he uses the hunting episode as the basis of a new symbolic theme, and he comments "subjectively" on the feelings of Aeneas. To take the subjective comment first, after reporting Aeneas' speech, Vergil describes the hero as follows: "sick with his tremendous cares, he pretends to hope by his expression, imprisoning deep in his heart the pain he feels" (208–9). Here Vergil shows how Aeneas aligns himself with the forces of Order, though subject to the disturbances that prompt Juno and others to violence. Instead of yielding to his "sickness," Aeneas represses it, checks it exactly as a leader should repress signs of disorder in himself or his subjects. Soon after he receives for the first time the epithet *pius* (221), as he expresses his misery in silent lamenting for his lost comrades. Vergil chose these comments because he wanted us to see the tension under which Aeneas operates and to realize the price he pays for his apparent serenity.

The new symbolic theme emerging from the deer-hunting is an ironic one. Like Odysseus, Aeneas brings food back to his men; unlike Odysseus, by this first act in Carthaginian territory he initiates a series of progressively more violent and destructive deeds which eventuate in the death of Queen Dido. The ambivalence of this first moment characterizes Aeneas' whole sojourn in Africa. He cannot advance his own cause without hurting Dido. Thus later the affair with this lovely woman will proceed amid hunting symbols: Aeneas first possesses Dido during a hunt; her passion for him is cast in terms of the agony of a wounded deer (4.69 ff.); and she herself wildly imagines herself as the quarry hunted down by Aeneas (4.465). Everything that Aeneas does seems to have its cruel price; every time he promotes the destined future he also hurts the present condition of someone else. Dido is Aeneas' victim and she anticipates the pathetic destiny of Carthage, doomed to be eradicated because it would stand in the way of Rome.

After the tired sailors fall asleep, Vergil uses the moment to transport us briefly to Olympus and elaborate the situation in cosmic terms through a conversation between Venus and Jupiter. We have already discussed Jupiter's great prediction. Early the next morning, Aeneas, who alone has passed a sleepless night worrying about the situation (305), sets out to reconnoiter. Before he gets far he encounters a huntress—or rather Venus his mother, who seems to him a huntress. It is a poignant meeting, for Aeneas does not realize until too late that he is talking with his mother, and she refuses to present herself directly. Why this should be so has never been clearly articulated by critics, and possibly it is better to leave the question to the reader's imagination. We might, however, note certain aspects of the scene. First of all, since it is not common for Venus to adopt hunting dress, we may assume that Vergil saw something particularly relevant in it. It might suggest the extent to which even his own mother compels Aeneas to be impersonal.

It might also indicate, in line with the other hunting motifs to which I have referred, the distorted way Aeneas himself views this new land and its people; he can see only hunters. Thus at first sight of Dido he imagines the beauteous huntress goddess Artemis (498 ff.). Replying to his inquiries, Venus seems to confirm my suggestion that her special garb in some way introduces Dido, for she asserts that girls from Tyre (Dido's original home) regularly dress as huntresses. In the second place, the cruel distance placed between mother and son indicates the way Vergil views the relation of gods and men. Whereas Homer gave Odysseus an Athena to serve as guide, companion, and friend, Venus, who here replaces Athena, cannot approach Aeneas, son though he is, except in disguise. As Vergil seems to imply, then, gods do help men, but rarely are men able to perceive this assistance or to feel it as special personal benevolence.

The help that Venus affords Aeneas is considerable: she predicts the safe return of his missing twelve ships, and she explains, both for him and for us, the background of Dido's settlement of Carthage. Dido, once of Tyre, lost her husband under tragic circumstances, then fled from her homeland leading a resolute band of her people. Once arrived in Carthage, she guided her followers in a stable and promising settlement. It is no accident that Dido's experiences will prove to resemble those of Aeneas, which we and she will hear about in Book Two. Vergil has deliberately brought together two people who have suffered similar misfortunes, dedicated themselves to founding new cities, and now, as they labor toward this political goal, feel the lack of a companion to fill out their private existence. The fact that Aeneas is a widower with a young son, longing to settle down in a comfortable home, explains why he quickly falls in love with beautiful Dido; and the fact that she is a childless young widow, who barely knew what marriage was like before the murder of her first husband, explains why she is vulnerable to handsome Aeneas and the boyish appeal of Ascanius (or Cupid disguised as Ascanius). It would seem, at first sight, like an ideal union; such a friendly resolution of international frictions would have prevented the Carthaginian Wars. But Fate cannot permit either Aeneas or Dido to follow freely a private romance.

Aeneas hears the facts about Dido without comment, then after bitter realization of his mother's elusive presence, pushes on toward Carthage. Wonder and envy strike him as he looks at the new city, for he wishes he were able to build his city. Shrouded in a god-given mist (like Odysseus entering Phaeacia), he proceeds toward the center of the city, finally pausing at an imposing temple dedicated to Juno. Although a temple of Juno might have worried him had he known the extent of her hostility, Aeneas finds comfort and hope there. Dido's artists have decorated the temple with panels—painted or in relief—which show sympathetically the events of the Trojan War—not merely the glorious victory of the Greeks (as Juno would have wanted), but also the heroism of the Trojans and the pathetic incidents which they experienced, such as the death of young Troilus and the ransoming of Hector's corpse by Priam. Aeneas senses in these artistic representations a humanity and sympathy which he has not often experienced since Troy's fall; it is in connection with these that he utters his famous phrase: *sunt lacrimae rerum* (462). Here, he thinks, people weep for others' misfortunes. Indeed, Dido is more than predisposed to pity him; the irony is that he will ultimately be prevented from acting humanely toward her, no matter how great his pity for her. Perhaps the setting in the temple of savage Juno acts as a sardonic comment on both these poor passionate mortals.

Vergil brings Aeneas before one final picture, then suddenly introduces Dido. The picture represents the Amazon Penthesilea raging (*furens*) and fierily active among men; Dido enters, surrounded by men, eager to press on with her political tasks and entirely rational—at this initial moment. Similarity and contrast. Dido is not now Penthesilea, but the tragic death of the frenzied Amazon is destined to be Dido's, and the juxtaposition of the two women is a skillful instance of Vergilian foreshadowing. At the moment, though, the contrast prevails. To capture the lovely, queenly aspects of Dido, Vergil reports that Aeneas sees her as regal Diana among her maidens. He describes Dido as an ideal ruler, presiding over a court, issuing just laws, and fairly allocating the tasks of the new city. To complete the favorable impression made upon Aeneas and us, men from Aeneas' "lost" twelve ships appear, appeal to Dido for humane treatment, and receive the warmest, most gracious hospitality. Not only is she willing to welcome the Trojans temporarily before sending them on their way richly loaded with gifts, but she also offers to settle them in Carthage, uniting them without any discrimination with her Tyrians. All that remains is for her to express a desire to meet Aeneas, and the hero, seeing that he indeed has reached an ideal environment, emerges from his concealment and identifies himself.

The honest enthusiasm of the moment makes Aeneas ardently swear that he will always honor Dido's name, no matter where he

may go. In fact, he probably does continue to honor her patheti-
cally, but the ultimate necessity of his departure for that settlement
in Rome forces from Dido a curse (4.622 ff.) that ironically answers
this oath. Oath and curse constitute the frame of the whole tragic
relationship. While Dido institutes preparations for a formal state
reception, Aeneas sends back to his ships to summon his son and
some gifts for the queen (647 ff.). Both gifts are emblematic of Dido's
fate, particularly a wedding veil which adulterous Helen brought
to Troy from Sparta. As for Ascanius, Venus has other plans. She
substitutes in his place Cupid (who is Aeneas' divine brother), with
the intention that Dido, attacked at her most vulnerable point—
her frustrated maternal desires—shall succumb to love of Ascanius
and, through him, to passion for Aeneas. Dido's love will then guar-
antee Aeneas and the Trojans security as long as they remain in
Carthage.

I have deliberately slanted the truth here to present Venus' in-
tentions in a solely positive, maternal light. Vergil aims at a differ-
ent interpretation and, by his use of imagery and subjective com-
ment, obliges us to question the validity of Venus' "loving" activi-
ties. Even if Venus does fear treacherous intervention from Juno—
a likely event as the Storm proves—her cruel manipulation of Dido
does not endear her to us. The imagery is the established series for
disorder: Cupid is to insinuate fire in Dido's bones, set her ablaze,
and drive her to fury (659–60). He must capture her before Juno
does, using treachery, and ring her with flame (673). After deceiving
her, he should breathe fire into her and trick her with poison (688).
This ought to suffice to predispose us in Dido's favor, for her inno-
cent love is being twisted by malevolent deities so that it burns her
up, sickens her, poisons her, and finally makes her a total captive
of her enemy. Each of these images functions powerfully in Book
Four, where Vergil works out Dido's tragedy.[2] To confirm our sym-
pathy for Dido here Vergil uses his subjective techniques. The de-
tails and acts which he assigns to Dido dominate our attention, and
above all her epithets guide our reactions. When Aeneas first saw
her, she was "absolutely beautiful" (*pulcherrima*, 496); and at the
beginning of the reception she is expected to be "radiantly happy"
(*laetissima*, 685). But under the influence of the "disease" started by
Cupid, she becomes pathetic (*infelix*, 712, 749) and wretched (*mis-
era*, 719). Not that Dido realizes what has happened to her or by
what divine forces she is being exploited; but Vergil intends us to
feel from the start the cruel fate to which Dido is exposed.

The banquet, which Vergil has designed as the dramatic setting for the end of Book One and for the long story of earlier events which Aeneas narrates in Books Two and Three, is normally a place of total festivity. Vergil makes the scene ironic. We may compare with this the Phaeacian banquet at which Odysseus tells his story: whereas the Phaeacians enjoy his tale and no ruinous passion results for Phaeacian Nausicaa, in Carthage Dido falls more and more under the spell of her charming guest and his insidiously appealing child. Her sympathy only increases her later pathetic suffering. Thus it is with mixed feelings that we hear *infelix Dido* eagerly request Aeneas to recount his past. That introduces and colors our attitude toward Book Two.

As we move from Book One to Book Two, we might well pause briefly to consider a central feature of Vergil's art—his structural techniques. Following the Homeric principle which Horace later codified as that of plunging the audience into the middle of the action (*in medias res*), Vergil depicted Aeneas in Book One sailing, he thought, toward his destined home along the west coast of Italy when suddenly Juno's diabolical storm sweeps the fleet far off course to Carthage. A long delay ensues before Aeneas can resume his trip. Books One and Four describe the temptation created by Dido and Aeneas' reluctant decision in the end to break away from her. Between Books One and Four, creating suspense by the interruption, Vergil placed Books Two and Three, books which serve the further purpose of establishing the background for Aeneas' pathetic adventure in Carthage. To a highly sympathetic Dido, overly susceptible to each sorrow that Aeneas has suffered, the Trojan tells how he lost his wife and city, how he has wandered far in weary search for that ever-receding promised home. The story accordingly explains Aeneas to us and simultaneously propels Dido ever closer toward her tragic passion. To grasp the extent of Vergil's economy here we need only recall that the *Odyssey*, the obvious prototype for much of Books One through Three, devoted eight books to similar material. It took Odysseus four books (Five through Eight) to sail through storms to Phaeacia, make his way to the court, and there, at a banquet, raise the curiosity of Alcinous so as to be forced to tell his story; then another four books (Nine through Twelve) are used while the skillful raconteur spellbinds his audience with his fantastic adventures. Moreover, Homer did not use the story as a means of furthering a tragic romance; at the end of his story Odysseus is really at the end of his wanderings, ready to be transported quickly back across the remaining sea to the coast of Ithaca. Aeneas has no such luck.

Vergil's structural genius has proved a rich and controversial field for recent scholarship.[3] I have already outlined one method of analyzing Books One through Four. In a similar fashion, Books Five through Eight can be described as a coherent unit which concentrates on the destiny of Rome; and Books Nine through Twelve form an intelligible whole: the defeat of Italian hopes and the tragic death of Turnus. Thus it is profitable to describe the *Aeneid* in terms of three sets of four books, to note that the great future of Rome is framed by the tragedies that it produces: that of Dido (Carthage) and that of Turnus (Italian foes of Roman expansion). I have also commented on the significant manner in which Vergil divided his epic, using the *Odyssey* as his archetypal pattern in Books One through Six, the *Iliad* in Seven through Twelve. Another useful pattern has been observed in the pairs of odd- and even-numbered books and I have myself chosen that grouping for my discussion of the *Aeneid* in this volume. The ardent spirit which Aeneas finds in this newly created Carthage contrasts poignantly with the feeling of defeat which emerges from his account of Troy's fall in Book Two; and the long frustrating search for a home, about which he speaks in Book Three, is passionately dramatized in the tragic events of Book Four. In these pairs of books, it has been noted, the even-numbered books tend to reach an emotional and dramatic height far beyond that of the corresponding odd-numbered books. The reader will be well repaid for his attempts to analyze the architectural patterns of the *Aeneid,* for Vergil clearly wrote with the sophisticated art that saw and emphasized recurring situations and themes. For example, when the second half of the *Aeneid* opens, he deliberately evoked memories of Book One and the disruptive character of Juno; he shows Juno first in angry soliloquy over the peaceful situation of the Trojans, then in violent action to cause a war which is the analogue of the storm of Book One. Again, Book Twelve frequently reminds us of elements of Book One, themes which Vergil at last brings to a conclusion.

It is furthermore very useful to analyze the structure of each book, for Vergil carefully worked it out to a significant form. Indeed some scholars have been so impressed by Vergilian artistry in this respect that they have attributed to him a precise mathematical symmetry; they have analyzed books and individual passages, counting the lines, and emerged with the thesis that Vergil adopted a principle of proportionality known as the Pythagorean golden mean.[4] I doubt that we need go so far as that; the image of Vergil writing poetry according to a mathematical formula does not improve our appreciation of his art. But Vergil did plan each book, just as he constructed his sets of books, to develop his themes in the most effective manner. We are not wrong, therefore, to use the metaphors of architecture and describe him as "building" his epic. Only we must resist the temptation to schematize Vergil's techniques and so detect our scheme (not his) at every point. With that warning I may tentatively suggest one pattern for Book One: 34–304 (the first day, Aeneas' arrival in Carthage and its place in Jupiter's ultimate plans); 305–578 (Aeneas explores Carthage and discovers the friendly character of its queen); 579–756 (Dido receives Aeneas, an act of generosity which malign forces exploit to start destroying her). Other legitimate patterns have been detected; this one, however, does illustrate the way Vergil develops his narrative from the storm, where homeless, friendless Aeneas became a plaything of vindictive Juno, to the ironically happy banquet in Carthage, where Aeneas enjoys a momentary, cruelly costly rest among generous friends.

If there is controversy about the dominant structural pattern of Book One, there is general agreement about Book Two. Three sections may be defined, although the poetic mastery of Vergil in transitions may cause readers some hesitation in placing the exact limits of the sections. Vergil first has Aeneas tell how the Trojans were deceived by the treacherous, lying Greeks and the malignant gods, with the result that they took into Troy the fatal Trojan Horse; I should close that section at 249. Next Aeneas recounts the vain struggle to defend the city against the Greek invader, a struggle which reaches its climax in the palace of King Priam; I end that section with Priam's death at 558. The final section describes how Aeneas succeeded in escaping the flames of his beloved Troy and indicates the hope that lies in the future for the Trojan remnants. It is not accidental that these sections have a rough numerical relationship—the first and third being approximately 250 lines each —but nothing is gained, I believe, by pressing the point too far. The truly important feature of these three sections is the way Vergil has used them to work out his manifold themes.[5]

The non-Roman tradition, which Homer represents so powerfully, treats the Trojans as guilty, the Greeks as "crusaders" carrying out the will of the gods and so justly victorious. The Roman tradition, which derived its founders from the Trojans, tended to minimize Trojan guilt and build up the pathos of Troy's fall, as well as the heroism of such survivors as Aeneas. Elaborating upon this Roman tradition, Vergil pictures the Trojans as humane, innocent people, exposed to Greek treachery by their own innocence, and further doomed by the malignant intervention of Minerva. He gains force for this view by expressing it through Aeneas, whose passionate involvement we are ready to understand, if not to adopt. It is crucial in Book Two to see how Aeneas participates in the events he reports.

The drama of Troy's deception has always been regarded as a masterpiece. Throughout the section our attention focuses on the Trojan horse—the means by which the treacherous Greeks gain entry into Troy, the symbol of Greek dishonesty. When the Trojans roved through the empty Greek encampment and found this horse, they did not know what to do with it. Laocoön's vigorous action failed to persuade them, doomed as they were. Far more effective were the lying words of Greek Sinon, who swore that the horse would, if taken into Troy, give the Trojans magic power over the Greeks. Then Minerva decided matters by causing the excruciating death of Laocoön and his sons. Deceived by Sinon, the Trojans also misinterpreted the death of Laocoön as punishment for sin. Minerva was indeed punishing Laocoön—for interfering with her plans to destroy Troy, which was his only "sin." Having inferred that the horse was a sacred object meant to bless Troy, the deluded Trojans declared a holiday and joyfully dragged the huge beast (and its load of hidden Greeks) into their city. On this ironic note of festivity, with nightfall, the section ends.

To enhance the power of his drama Vergil develops an intricate symbolic pattern here. Deception, the major theme, is practiced by Sinon, epitomized by the horse with its hidden armed men, and vividly symbolized by the snakes that consume Laocoön. And Vergil makes sure that we feel the links between these seemingly separate aspects of deception. When we study the language used to describe the snakes in 203 ff., we note a series of words which have already been used to describe actions of the Greeks and particularly of Sinon. Thus the snakes come from Tenedos, precisely where the Greeks lurk, ready to return as soon as the horse enters Troy. The very name Sinon is echoed in the Latin word for coils (*sinus*) and the verb for sinuous motion; Sinon, in other words, is a "snake." When the snakes kill Laocoön, Aeneas tells us that terror "slithered into" (*insinuat,* 229) the Trojan hearts; they were deceived as to the meaning of the death. The snakes escape to take refuge on the citadel in the shrine of Minerva, and soon the horse is dragged up to the same spot, its symbolic identity with the snakes suggested by the unusual words which Vergil uses to represent its movement —as if it too slithered along!

Although deception is the major significance of the snakes at first, Vergil makes it clear by means of the death scene of Laocoön that the deception aims at violent destruction of Troy. The agony of Laocoön will soon be matched by that of thousands of Trojans, the victims of that horse and the many Greeks who, like the snakes, will cross from Tenedos and enter Troy. Vergil effectively adds to his description of the serpents metaphors of blood and fire: their crests are blood-red, their eyes ablaze with blood and fire. In the next section, blood, fire, and snake imagery combine to bring out the horror of Troy's destruction.

During the deception section, Aeneas played no important part. Others like Laocoön and Priam had significant roles, but Aeneas the narrator does not individualize himself at all. We may imagine him, if we wish, wandering through the empty Greek camp; Vergil limits Aeneas to an occasional first person plural, which shows that the hero was but part of the nameless crowd (see 25, 105, 212, 234, 248) when Sinon was interviewed, when the snakes killed Laocoön, and when the Trojans brought the horse into Troy. One of the signs that a new section starts is not only the second reference to the Greeks on Tenedos (255), but the sudden importance of Aeneas, now mentioned in the first person singular (271). From this point Aeneas the narrator is highly conscious of his experiences and we are made aware of his role as leader of Trojan resistance, potential leader of Trojan destiny.

The first episode involving Aeneas deserves our attention. It opens with the snake metaphor: sleep, like a snake, a "gift of the gods," as Vergil ironically puts it, had wound its way into the Trojans. In this ruinous sleep, Aeneas dreamed that Hector, the mainstay of Troy until his death, came to him, dissuaded him from further resistance, and entrusted him with Troy's future in the form of the sacred emblems, which Aeneas was to carry across the sea to a new city. Significant as this "commission" is to us, it made no immediate impression upon Aeneas. Not until he saw Priam fall was he ready to believe that Troy was finished, that he might try to escape. Vergil captures the moment that Aeneas awoke and slowly realized the Trojan disaster in a particularly brilliant manner, using a pastoral simile (304 ff.). From his rooftop, viewing the fires blazing up in the darkness, hearing the shrieks of the dying, Aeneas was like a shepherd on a hilltop, watching in the distant valley below a flame rage through the crops or a torrent sweep over fields. The comparison, which reminds one of Lucretius and, to some extent, of the world of the *Eclogues,* depicts Aeneas in what the Epicureans would have considered the ideal condition—uninvolved. Aeneas, too, frequently would like to escape his destiny and break free of involvement with Troy's future; but he never yields to this Epicurean temptation of social and political disengagement for long. In this instance, entirely unaware that he is committing himself forever, Aeneas races down from his roof and into desperate battle. He will, if anything, be a "shepherd" of his people.

Aeneas passionately commits himself to battle, more than eager to die with his city. To convey the general confusion and violence of the situation and to affect our attitude about war in general, Vergil exploits the dramatic possibilities of nighttime and the symbols which he established in the first section. Fire rages everywhere, and the uneven light of the flames provides the main illumination for the scene. In the semidarkness Aeneas, with a small band of Trojans, falls in with a Greek detachment, catches it unawares, and destroys it. Then, seizing the opportunity, the Trojans put on the Greek armor. So disguised they kill many Greeks and spread consternation, but not for long. Vergil uses a snake simile to interpret the situation (379 ff.); and this time the Trojans are "snakes." Anyone who tries underhand methods of fighting, Greek or Trojan, is a "snake." Soon the Greeks penetrate the disguise, and simultaneously Aeneas' band becomes the target of Trojan spears. Aeneas escapes with but two men toward the center of resistance, Priam's palace, and mounts to the roof to join in the defense. From there he watches the ruinous actions of the Greek Pyrrhus, also compared to a vigorous snake by Vergil (471 ff.). True son of Achilles, Pyrrhus is first to break into the palace; he hurries through the rooms, kills Priam's son, then butchers the king himself on the altar. The act epitomizes the sacrilegious violence of the Greeks and the fall of Troy. Aeneas can do nothing further. He has come from his own rooftop through the enemy to Priam's rooftop; now he pauses to think of his own family, having seen what happened to Priam.

The final section starts from that moment of utter despair and works toward an ending of hope, in which the destructive symbols of snakes, fire, and divine antagonism are converted into happy symbols pointing to a glorious future for New Troy (Rome) in a new land. The night of terror ends as Aeneas escapes from the city; a new day dawns at 801 ff., another emblem of hope. At the beginning, though, the situation is grim, so grim that the other Trojans around Aeneas have taken the path of desperation and hurled themselves suicidally from the palace roof. The question for Aeneas is: what should *he* do? Unfortunately, at this precise point the early

manuscripts of the *Aeneid* face us with the problem of guessing
Vergil's intentions. All of these manuscripts proceed directly from
that scene of despair to the intervention of Venus (from 566 to 589
in our conventional numbering). Servius, however, who reports oc-
casionally upon the action of the *Aeneid's* editors, tells us that they
omitted twenty-two lines, which he proceeds to cite in full. In these
lines Aeneas says that he suddenly spied Helen and, in a surge of
fury, decided to avenge upon her the ruin of Troy and the deaths
of so many Trojans. Did Vergil write these lines? The answer seems
to be yes, with the crucial qualification that the whole passage
seems defective, below the usual Vergilian stage of polish. Did the
editors delete them? Again, yes. Did they do it on their own deci-
sion, or did they follow some hint from Vergil? There is the real
problem. I myself believe that Vergil would have revised this pas-
sage, but left it essentially unchanged in the text; the reader should
decide this issue himself. Here are a few points to consider. The
unfinished quality of the passage may have been marked by Vergil.
The editors may have seized upon that as justification for excising
a passage which on other grounds—namely, Aeneas' unchivalrous
attitude toward a woman—embarrassed them. On the other hand,
Vergil may have wished to emphasize the low state of Aeneas' pas-
sions so as to enhance, by contrast, the confidence with which the
hero eventually leaves Troy. Aeneas' search for a scapegoat is en-
tirely natural; it is also the kind of spontaneous passion which
must be forsaken if Rome is to be built. Finally, if we compare this
scene with the death of Turnus in Book Twelve, we may perceive
more clearly Vergil's intentions with the whole epic in the distinc-
tion between killing Helen in futile fury and killing Turnus in a
fury that contains within itself the tragedy of all history.[6]

Venus, preventing Aeneas from his vengeance, directs him home-
ward after revealing to him the extent of divine opposition to
Troy's existence. If Priam's Troy is doomed, though, something can
still be rescued and transplanted elsewhere: that is Aeneas' mission.
Back at his palace, more despair meets him. His father Anchises
wishes to perish with Troy, for life has no further meaning, he
believes. As Aeneas once again yields to his emotions, rushing to-
ward the door and violent death in battle, a miracle occurs that
transforms everyone's despair into hope. A tongue of flame appears
on Ascanius' head, licking around his locks with movements that
might well remind us of Laocoon's snakes, with the crucial differ-
ence that this flame is harmless (681 ff.). It cannot be extinguished
by normal means, so it is god-given, but it does not burn the child.

Anchises is the first to react: his despair becomes joy, and with eagerness he prays to Jupiter to confirm his happy interpretation of the omen. At that, across the sky streaks a comet, "sliding" over Troy (like a snake), hiding itself (again like a snake) in the forests of Mt. Ida outside the city. Anchises knows the meaning: the gods have picked his grandson to continue Troy elsewhere, a Troy that will not fall to flames or deception, a Troy which will have destiny on its side. And it is Anchises' duty to further that end as long as he lives.

Grandfather, son, and grandson leave burning Troy together, grouped by Vergil to bring out the way the burden rests mainly upon Aeneas to establish that happy future.[7] Creusa, Aeneas' wife, loses her way and disappears. When Aeneas risks his life and Troy's future to find her, the gods step in again to check his passionate indulgence. A vision of Creusa stresses once again, as Hector did earlier, that Aeneas has a mission (776 ff.); he will suffer and be obliged to wander far before at last reaching Hesperia and finding a new wife. There is little personal comfort in such words—apart from the fact that Aeneas learns of Creusa's place among the gods —but Aeneas is never to have comfort, only responsibility and the assurance that his actions advance New Troy. Accepting this duty, Aeneas proceeds with the dawn toward the goal marked out by the comet, Mt. Ida. From there, in Book Three, he will commence his long search for Hesperia.

⤳ III ⤳

THE SEARCH FOR HOME: BOOKS
THREE AND FOUR

Book Three continues Aeneas' narrative, and Book Four continues
the experiences of Aeneas in Carthage until his departure causes
heartache to himself and tragedy to Dido. Although it might seem
that Three has closer links to Two and Four to One, Vergil has
planned his sequence purposefully—for, in fact, Three and Four
are interrelated with particular skill. The leading motif of both
books can be given the title I have selected above: the search for
home. Aeneas faces two crucial questions: where is his destined
home and what will be its essential character? In Book Three, after
many false starts, he finally learns the location of his future home:
Italy. But we watch him in Book Four cherishing a false home,
Carthage, and reluctantly assenting to the god's command to give
it up for Italy. In Book Three Aeneas slowly and painfully realizes
that his new home cannot be a facsimile of Troy; in Book Four
he finds that Carthage, no matter how unique and different from
Troy, cannot be his destined settlement. His home permits him no
personal pleasure, certainly not the passionate relation he had en-
joyed with Dido. Thus we can schematize the relation of these two
books in terms of Aeneas' long, weary search for his destined coun-
try. In Book Three Aeneas moves out of the old world of enmity
between Troy and Greece into a world where he can befriend a
Greek, Achaemenides. At the end, with the death of Anchises,
Aeneas becomes total master of the expedition. In Book Four
Aeneas makes his first important stop in the new world. The result
is tragically significant. Whereas in the old world Aeneas and the
Trojans were victims, it now seems that Aeneas' destiny creates
victims. Dido is only the first.

I BOOK THREE

Book Three consists of a series of arrivals and departures, but
the episode to which Vergil devotes the most attention occurs sig-

nificantly at the center of the book (291–505). Instead of going through the book episode by episode, I shall concentrate on this central scene and show how Vergil employs it to work out his primary themes. In the first third of Book Three, Aeneas rapidly summarizes his failures to found a new city in the familiar Greco-Trojan world (1–290); in the final third (506–718) he describes his first frightening experiences in the new world of Italy. Placed in the middle of these swift adventures, the central episode allows us and Aeneas time to grasp its pivotal significance.[1]

Vergil has obviously selected the locale for this scene with care, exploiting myths which his predecessors had either ignored or left unstressed when following the wanderings of Aeneas. Buthrotum, the city to which Aeneas brings his fleet at 293, lies on the coast of Epirus, an area north of Greece proper and never more than half-Greek at any time in antiquity. As if to confirm the non-Greek quality of the place, Vergil tells us that the Greek ruler of the region, savage Pyrrhus (killer of Priam), has been murdered at Delphi and replaced in power not by Greeks, but by Trojans, Helenos and Andromache. On the periphery of the Greek world, then, but ruled by Trojans, Buthrotum offers a pleasant stop to Aeneas' weary men; it cannot be a permanent stop, for as it soon appears, Buthrotum functions as Aeneas' port of departure for Italy and his destined home. Less than one-hundred miles of the Ionian Sea separate Aeneas from his first landfall in Italy. Utilizing Buthrotum's geographical position as the basis of his interpretation, Vergil shows how Aeneas arrives physically and psychologically at the point where he can make the break from the old world to the new.

The basic pattern of arrival and departure permits infinite variations in artistic treatment. When Aeneas reaches Buthrotum, he has no preliminary knowledge of its character, friendly or hostile. But he soon discovers that his own people dominate the place, a fact which he rapidly confirms when he encounters Andromache, widow of heroic Trojan Hector, outside the city. A tearful reunion here is followed by triumphal entry within the walls, as the Trojans are escorted by the king-prophet, Trojan Helenos. Nevertheless, although they find themselves in this loving and long-desired Trojan environment, Aeneas and his men do not remain long, only long enough to secure a prophecy from Helenos about their approaching adventures in Italy. Then amid tears they sail. This seemingly uncomplex, uneventful episode, which Vergil expands by using much direct speech, contrasts sharply with the preceding episodes.

Despite the prophecies of Hector and Creusa (reported in Book Two), Aeneas had no intention of seeking a distant, vaguely defined settlement. He first sailed the short distance across the Bosporus and landed in supposedly friendly territory in Thrace. However, when he began his new city he discovered that this land was not only hostile but also accursed, tainted by the murder of the youngest son of Priam. The branches which he intended to employ to sanctify the new site dripped ominous gore: obviously Troy could not be revived in Thrace. The pattern of the "friendly" place which turns accursed and frustrates hope of settlement repeats itself in Crete. Hither the Trojans think they have been directed by prophecy (later more correctly interpreted), and everything seems in their favor. In Crete again, after a promising start to the new city called Pergamea (a reminder of Troy), plague strikes the Trojans and indicates a new curse. They must leave.

Thrace and Crete, both intended to be settlements copying (hence named after) Troy, turn hostile after an initial peaceful reception. We might have expected a repetition of this pattern at Buthrotum, but the fact is that Buthrotum does not drive away the band of Aeneas. It remains hospitable; they, on their own, determine to forsake its friendly environment for the unknown perils of Italy. What has changed the pattern? In the first place, Aeneas has at last grasped the fact that his destination is Italy, not any other site in the Aegean or near the Greek coast on the west. Intimately connected with the tragic failures in Thrace and Crete is an ambiguous prophecy which he received in Delos: his destination, the oracle of Apollo declared, was the original "motherland" of the Trojans (94 ff.). Since Thrace was not the motherland, the prophecy helped to explain the failure there. It was Anchises who rushed to the conclusion that Crete was the intended motherland, for Teucer, a Trojan ancestor, had come from there. The plague in Crete proved Anchises wrong, and he proposed returning to Delos to clarify the original prophecy: he himself could not help. At this point Apollo intervened, sending a dream message to Aeneas, not Anchises, and explaining that the "motherland" belonged to the other Trojan ancestor Dardanus, who originated in Italy. Knowing from this profound personal experience where his destination lies, Aeneas no longer deceives himself when he reaches friendly Buthrotum, nor does he depend on his father to define his goal. Since he accepts the fact that Buthrotum is not a possible settlement, he does not need to be expelled by plague or other divine omen. It costs him deep sorrow to part from his friends, but he goes unhesitantly.

There is a second significance in Aeneas' unhesitant departure from Buthrotum: he has gradually learned something about the nature of his destined settlement. Not only will it be located in Italy, in the new world, but it will necessarily be different from Troy. At Buthrotum Helenos and Andromache have succeeded in creating a facsimile of Troy, and since the gods have no better purposes for them, they have permitted this imitation to survive. But Aeneas now sees it for what it is: a toy Troy, with a miniscule copy of the mighty citadel Pergama, a dried-up stream named after the majestic river Xanthus, a fake Simois, and unimpressive gates patterned on Troy's Scaean Gates (349 ff.). This pathetic facsimile has no life or future at all. Its prevailing mood is tears; its attention is fixed on the dead past; and its symbol is the cenotaph of Hector by which Aeneas finds Andromache weeping as he approaches the walls. There is no child of Andromache—the Greeks killed him at Troy—to continue Trojan greatness in Buthrotum, and Vergil pointedly ignores the young people of the town. It has no future, only a tragic dead past to stir its feelings.

In discerning the location and the nature of his "motherland," Aeneas has also discovered himself. Vergil does not decisively define the time it took to reach this haven after leaving Troy, but he more than once implies that seven years have elapsed.[2] In that period Aeneas has gradually established himself as the undisputed leader, while gently freeing himself from dependence on his beloved father. He had abandoned Thrace only after consulting the Trojan leaders, particularly his father. He had gone to Crete because Anchises convinced him (erroneously) that Crete was the prophesied "motherland." But then comes the dream from Apollo, received only by himself. From that moment, he no longer needs to consult Anchises, nor does the old man play any further important role. When the Trojans arrive at the westernmost point of Sicily, ready to sail the last stretch of sea to Cumae, Vergil adopts a useful tradition—not the universal one—according to which Anchises dies, worn out with the long journey.[3] Anchises belonged to the past and, though compelled to assent to the Trojan future in the new world, he himself could not personally adapt to it. Like Moses barred from the promised land, the patriarch of the Trojans was prevented from participating in the new settlement. Although Aeneas will succumb to some temptations at first, in theory he now requires no parental guidance; the destiny of the New Troy depends entirely upon him.

I do not think it an accident that Vergil reminds us of the proximity of Buthrotum and Phaeacia. According to one common ancient tradition, Homer's Phaeacia could be identified with the island of Corcyra off the coast of Epirus. Vergil admired, no doubt, the way Homer made Phaeacia a halfway point on Odysseus' journey back from the remote island of Calypso to Ithaca; by reminding us of that sojourn here, he invites us to compare the halfway point he has assigned to Aeneas. Just as Odysseus emerges from a series of personal tests to his self-indulgence and, landing at Phaeacia, remains immune to temptation (and so demonstrates his readiness to proceed to the final test at home), so Aeneas has come through trials that affect his people as much as himself. What he suffers is for the benefit of New Troy. Just as Odysseus refuses to stop for long in Phaeacia despite an obvious opportunity to marry the royal princess, so Aeneas rejects the comforts of this friendly Trojan atmosphere. It costs him more to leave Buthrotum, but he has a destiny beyond himself to fulfil.

One final point requires some comment, namely, the link between Book Three and Book Four, between the story which Aeneas here tells to Dido and the experiences which he and Dido will share to their tragic end. Not only can the arrival and departure pattern defined for Book Three be followed at Carthage, but also particular episodes of Book Three have analogues in Dido's life. To take briefly the first stop in Thrace, we learn that Thrace drives Aeneas away because in its soil is buried the secretly murdered Polydorus, whose gold has roused the vicious cupidity of his brother-in-law. Almost an identical crime drove Dido from her native Tyre: her brother murdered her rich husband Sychaeus in order to possess his gold. Naturally Dido would sympathize fully with Aeneas' plight, remembering her own. Another analogy is offered by Andromache, the lovely, pathetic wife of Hector. After Hector's death and a series of misfortunes occasioned by the fall of Troy, Andromache now shares the rule of Buthrotum. Does she develop qualities compatible with her new status? Not at all. She remains the unhappy woman she has been since she sent Hector out to his fatal battle with Achilles, not a regal figure making creative use of authority. Her tears for Hector as she first encounters Aeneas are matched by her laments for her dead son as she says farewell to the Trojans (and particularly Ascanius). What an obvious contrast Dido is despite her analogous misfortunes. She too has lost her dear husband, so early that she never even had a child by him. Yet she asserted her character, assumed command of the Tyrian exiles, and now has personally founded a vitally promising settlement in Africa. This admirable queen, who greets Aeneas so magnanimously, will become a victim of Aeneas' impersonal destiny and be reduced to a pathetic woman like Andromache, weeping at the departure of Aeneas, then killing herself.

II BOOK FOUR

By contrast with Book Three, we instantly note that the poet develops a rich fabric of imagery in Four.[4] The first lines focus our attention on the queen and interpret her state in terms of "wounds," destructive "fire," "disease," a metaphorical version of irrational passion (*cura*) which has been caused paradoxically by Aeneas' heroic qualities and the nobility of his race. With these initial metaphors Vergil not only establishes the tragic notes for Dido's relation with Aeneas, but also broaches the larger theme: Aeneas' nobility and the magnificent Rome for which he stands are always causing controversy and destruction, for no individual or nation can maintain its integrity whether hating or loving Aeneas. The second striking use of symbolism occurs in 66 ff., where Vergil enhances his metaphors of "fire" and "wounds" with a simile which now defines the kind of "wound" Dido has suffered. She resembles a deer which, after being struck by a shepherd's casual arrow, flees, wild with pain, through woods and groves. It is a highly sophisticated simile, for its Latin specifically evokes the first episode when Aeneas landed in Africa and shot down real deer (1.191 and 4.71), restates the hunting theme of Book One, applies the imagery of the opening of Four, and suggests the innocent involvement of Aeneas as the unconsciously cruel shepherd-huntsman. To dramatize the Fall of Dido Vergil ingeniously devises—it is undoubtedly his contribution to the myth, entirely consistent with his symbolism—a hunt where all attention concentrates upon Aeneas, who fells no victim until he follows Dido into a cave, driven by Juno's storm, and there causes, quite unconsciously of course, her inevitable ruin. Though Vergil remains silent about what went on in the cave— the prudent silence that belongs to a master poet alone—and thus does not permit us to say by what stages the affair proceeded, it does not take much imagination to picture these two lonely, handsome, passionate people, drawn with seeming inevitability, without conscious volition or guilt, into each other's arms.[5]

Unfortunately what for Dido is total commitment is for Aeneas love without the possibility of commitment. Vergil takes this basic situation of Greco-Roman tragedy, the different degrees of involvement of male and female lovers, and masterfully represents it by means of the hunt, the intervention of Juno and Venus, and the tragic irony of the so-called marriage in the cave. The whole hunting symbolism has been built up to make of Dido a pathetic victim of a cruelly indifferent, because unaware, hunter. That cannot possibly be twisted into the symbolism of "happy marriage"; Dido is ruined, not fulfilled, in the cave. Juno's intervention to produce this marriage has been pitilessly frustrated by that smiling, gentle mother of Aeneas—Venus, goddess of passionate love. It may seem to us at first that the interview between the two goddesses (90 ff.) exhibits markedly comic features, but Vergil masks his irony cleverly here. Venus holds all the cards; she has "disabled" or "conquered" Dido by passion, thus temporarily protecting Aeneas, and now she is willing to let that passion destroy Dido when Aeneas, as she knows he must, leaves Carthage. She agrees to the marriage, knowing that it cannot meet Jupiter's or fate's approval—as Juno, were she less irrational, should also know. When Juno engineers the marriage by shattering the ordered patterns of the hunt with a storm, her characteristic weapon of disorder (Vergil echoes in 160 the Latin of 1.124), we are expected to sense the ambiguity: this is no marriage but the beginning of Dido's destruction, unwittingly brought on by Dido's patron Juno.

There is an old controversy about Dido's "guilt" in all this. Especially in the nineteenth century, when marriage was often talked about—if not entirely treated—as something sacred, commentators rather glibly explained Dido's tragedy in terms of her perjured oath toward her first husband Sychaeus. We now recognize that such a view is neither realistic nor even consistent with ancient practices. Although dramatic characters frequently assert, as their mates are dying, that they will never remarry (and Vergil knew the motif well),[6] remarriage obviously did happen both in myth and normal Greek and Roman life. To remarry is both natural and politically astute, as Anna, Dido's sister, correctly argues. So Aeneas will remarry when he arrives in Italy, patently without the slightest stain on his reputation. The crucial fact is not that Dido "broke her faith" to Sychaeus, but that she entered into a pseudo-marriage which destroyed her honor. Despite all the apparent paraphernalia of Roman marriage ritual assembled by deluded Juno, the whole cave episode amounts to a mere travesty, a parody, in which Dido gives herself unreservedly (without asking for the protection of conventional marriage arrangements) and Aeneas gives himself with unspoken reservations. Dido certainly wins our sympathy for her commitment. At the same time we must recognize why Vergil labels this passion with destructive metaphors, because its irrational features lead Dido to disregard her total range of responsibilities, as well as those of Aeneas, and so to bring upon herself the consequences of an unreal "marriage." That, in the highest sense, is tragic "guilt."

One final tragic motif in the early lines of the book deserves comment. At least since the tragedies of Euripides it was conventional to motivate a heroine's fatal decision by her conversation with a down-to-earth confidante, usually the old family nurse. Phaedra's nurse, acting from honest concern, leads her to the abyss by making her think that something could be arranged with Hippolytos. Apollonius appropriated the motif in his epic *Argonautica,* working up a conversation between Medea and her sister about Medea's passion for Jason. Conventionally the advice is honestly given, the results tragic. *If* Aeneas had been able to marry Dido freely, then Anna would have been proved right. As it was, Anna released Dido from her restraints before ascertaining Aeneas' feelings. Vergil exploits the familiar motif to forewarn us, as he does by the initial imagery, of the impending tragedy for Dido. And his subjective comments on the religious rituals which follow Dido's "release" (65 ff.) make unmistakably clear the future course of action.

When public opinion (rumor) condemns the guilty pair's indulgence and Jupiter forcibly reminds Aeneas of prior responsibilities—nothing apparently deters Dido—Aeneas' immediate reaction is to obey instantly and unswervingly; his second reaction, which imposes a delay and should earn him some respect, is to consider his beloved Dido and the pain he will cause her. His main problem, then, is not leaving—that is certain—but how to make the necessary break with Dido with the minimum of pain to her. If we can forget the sentimental criticism of the nineteenth century, which still dogs classical studies, and recognize the situation for the basic human one it is, we should be able to see that it is far more poignantly tragic than the affair which Victorian critics imagined. Aeneas loves Dido more than any other human being, and his love lingers on after his departure (6.450 ff.), but he has other responsibilities, to family and people, which make pursuit of that love guilty indulgence. The same is true, of course, for Dido; but whereas Aeneas recognizes his larger moral responsibilities, Dido fails to see anything but the lesser, more immediate and obvious moral relationships established by love.

The long final tragic movement begins with a pair of balanced speeches, first Dido's, then Aeneas'. Dido's is introduced by a simile (300 ff.) which compares her to a bacchante racing wildly, fired to irrationality, through the town. The contrast with Aeneas' pained but controlled response to the necessity of departure is patent. Signs of irrationality appear here and there in her speech—as when she accuses Aeneas of intending to slip away without speaking to her, like a treacherous dog (305 ff.)—but for the most part she appeals for pity in the name of their love, and she deservedly wins sympathy. In fact, Aeneas does deeply pity and love her; Vergil's introduction (331 ff.) could not be more lucid on this point. However, he cannot indulge his feelings, and it would not be fair or even considerate to indulge Dido's appeal for pity, not if she is ever going to face the fact of his necessary going. The apparent coldness and rationality of his words; then, represents a heroic achievement on his part: the conquest of his own passion and the concerned desire to bring Dido back to reality. He talks facts, not feelings. They were not married, he insists, and he never tried to deceive her on this point. He cannot pursue his own desires because the gods and his sense of responsibility hound him across the seas—away from his beloved Troy, now away from his beloved Dido. "Love" for him has to focus on that distant, unknown home in Italy (347); normal human love, such as he feels for Dido, cannot prevail against that inhuman, abstract love, much as he would want it to. The sum of it is: "I seek Italy, but not of my own will." With that (361) his speech abruptly breaks off, and the hexameter line was left unfinished by Vergil. I believe that Vergil deliberately used the unorthodox break to suggest the true depth of Aeneas' feelings. His self-control had reached a breaking point, so he stopped rather than neatly round out his speech, a physical impossibility for him at the time.[7]

The seeming coolness of Aeneas only fires Dido; his rationality only begets irrationality in her. Her second speech (365 ff.) uses the conventional phrases of the abandoned woman to deny Aeneas all humanity, pour scorn on his reasonable statements, and finally allude to her imminent death (385). As if to confirm her complete lack of self-control, Vergil describes her sudden collapse at the end. Aeneas consequently cannot reply to her wild accusations, but must watch her being carried from the room unanswered, uncomforted. It is the last moment he sees her alive. With this dramatic interruption, Vergil destroys the balance of speeches. Aeneas cannot justify himself to Dido or restore her to rationality. Since Aeneas does possess self-control and has accepted his responsibilities, Vergil does not spend time magnifying this resoluteness, heroic though it is, by magniloquent soliloquies. Content to show the steady attitude of Aeneas by brief objective description, the poet lavishes detail on Dido, the tragic victim of this drama. Unfortunately, the Victorian blindness to genuine tragedy and propensity to warp all events into little sentimental situations of women wronged by caddish men has left us a heritage of misinterpretation of these scenes and of Vergil's artistic efforts. To be sure, he sympathized with Dido, as he will later sympathize with Turnus, Amata, and Mezentius, but not to the exclusion of reasonable judgment. He definitely did *not* consider Aeneas a "cad," and there is nothing in Book Four to justify such an attitude. Aeneas is not condemned by Dido's words, passionate though they may be; her unreasonable view of Aeneas' actions, her distortion of his motives, and the suicidal thoughts to which she is led all serve to dramatize her tragic moral collapse from the proud, controlled, benevolent queen she once was. And to decline from regal responsibility, as Vergil has emphasized by contrasting Aeolus with Neptune or Jupiter, is to risk ruining others and oneself, precisely what Dido is now doing. Thus the fact that Aeneas no longer addresses Dido, defends himself, or utters his passionate regrets *is* eloquent, but not in the sentimentally romantic way that the nineteenth century believed. He is unhappy for himself and Dido (395), but he does what should be done. On any reasonable moral balance, the choice between his beloved Dido and the destiny of his family and people is obvious; add to that the fact that he could not anticipate the extent of Dido's emotional breakdown or the suicide to which it would lead. Great poet and humanitarian that he is, Vergil registers the heavy price paid by Aeneas with profound pathos, but he expected his audience to distinguish intelligently, not sentimentally, between *infelix Dido,* tragic victim of her guilt and impossible circumstances, and *pius Aeneas,* unhappy, heroic servant of destiny who accepts the necessity of denying his own deepest emotions.[8]

Dido recovers from her faint and watches the activity of the Trojans as they prepare to sail. Instead of recalling her to her queenly functions by reminding her of the total inactivity of her Carthaginians resulting from her neglect (cf. 86 ff.), of those "busy bees" which Aeneas saw when first entering Carthage (see 1.423 ff. and 4.404 ff. for the contrasting similes), the Trojan bustle only drives her into more desperate speeches and passionate efforts to halt the inevitable. She sends Anna to appeal to Aeneas, not to give up his departure, but to postpone it until Spring guarantees easy sailing. Again Aeneas says nothing; there was nothing new for Vergil to have him say. But Aeneas remains the lover of Dido, wretched at her agony and unhappy to lose her; that he is able to maintain his self-control and obedience only by a struggle, Vergil makes clear. A magnificent simile (441 ff.) reveals his internal conflict. He resembles a huge, full-grown oak in the Alps assailed by violent north winds, losing leaves and branches, but clinging with its deep roots (that reach all the way to hell) to the crags and continuing to stand against the battering gales. Partly interpreting this comparison for us (447 ff.), the poet notes that Aeneas is battered by Dido's appeals and feels love and pity to the depth of his heart, but his purpose remains immovable even though his emotions express themselves in tears that roll from his eyes—all in vain (inanes). "Vain tears" are not crocodile tears. Far from condemning Aeneas with the phrase, Vergil tries to epitomize his impossible situation and to give him far more moral credit than tearful, broken Dido.

The last act is Dido's; Vergil eliminates Aeneas almost completely so that we can concentrate, with full sympathy, on this magnificent woman, fallen from noble queen to the pathetic state of helpless lover. In a paragraph (452 ff.) which describes evil omens and nightmares plaguing Dido, Vergil rounds off the previous section; Dido has disintegrated far beyond the bacchante of 300 ff. When she decides to commit suicide, we are not really surprised; suicide is the logical resolution for her wretched condition. Again, however, we must distinguish between the logical dramatical development of Dido's character, sympathetic as Vergil has rendered it, and the actions which a sane, self-controlled though deeply pained woman could have performed. We are not to view Dido as a stoic sage choosing the only intelligent, moral way out, hence committing a noble Catonian suicide. Her suicide is a confession, a manifestation of personal failure, and she knows it. Aeneas also made his mistakes in Carthage—betrayed his goal, ignored family, people, and gods' commands, and undoubtedly alienated all. However, he did not commit suicide, or even consider it. Just as he acted resolutely and selflessly, denying love, so Queen Dido could have resumed her position, profoundly sad but rationally facing facts. She didn't. When Aeneas sails, she falls upon his sword.

Vergil weaves many notes into the last moments of his tragedy.

There is rumor, which has helped to ruin Dido, now reporting her ruin. There is the simile which compares grief-stricken Carthage to a city conquered and sacked: this is the result of Aeneas' "unconscious hunting" and, in historical terms, will be the result of Rome's unplanned expansion in the Mediterranean. There is Anna, the wretched sister who sees where her advice has ended and laments helplessly. And finally there is Juno, perhaps the most pathetic of all, called *omnipotens* (693) with powerful irony, exhibiting for the first time a sympathy and almost maternal concern which have been most lacking so far in her personality. We need not ask what cruel Venus is doing. Vergil focuses our attention on the defeated victims of Roman destiny as Juno tenderly eases her favorite "child" through her final minutes: a picture of loving pity which suggests bleak thoughts about Aeneas' future.

❦ IV ❧

SICILY AND ITALY: BOOKS
FIVE AND SIX

As I indicated earlier, some writers analyze the *Aeneid* in "triads" of four books. If we give a backward glance now at the four books we have discussed, we can see the merits of considering them as a group. In Books One through Four Vergil develops the tragic story of Dido and Aeneas, inserting within it—both to help account for Aeneas' present condition and to establish some of the basic motifs recurring in the Carthaginian sojourn—Aeneas' narrative of Troy's fall and his long years of wandering in search of his new home. Both literally and figuratively Aeneas is blown off course to the coast of Africa, and so his experiences constitute a part of his unhappy wanderings, the most vivid and tragic because of the effective way that Vergil chooses to present them to us. The momentary pleasure in his false home, the violently broken attachment, and then the death of Dido constitute recurring parts of a fundamental pattern which continues into Book Five and, in a new way, into the first years in Italy. With Book Five, however, it is apparent that Vergil makes some new starts; this is rendered most obvious by the fact that he brings Aeneas back to the very port from which he was taken off course, Drepanum in Sicily, precisely one year from the day he lost Anchises. In Book Five, then, Aeneas returns literally and figuratively to his "course," for his recovery of stature as a leader, ready for the arduous adventures ahead in Italy, matches or parallels the physical move from Africa back to Sicily. The games which Aeneas celebrates in honor of his father almost suggest that he is holding the funeral of Anchises, as though the death had just occurred and no Carthaginian disaster had ever scarred the Trojan leader. Despite another setback caused by Juno in Sicily, Aeneas eventually gains the strength to sail onward, and the gods grant him an easy voyage at minimum cost: the life of Palinurus. Arrived at Cumae, Aeneas concludes his long wanderings on an essentially happy note. The protracted series of incomplete prophecies find their fulfillment in, first, the predictions of the Cumaean Sibyl,

then, the indefinable "experience" of the future that will result
from his seemingly unrewarded efforts. When he emerges from the
underworld, a thoroughly changed man, Aeneas looks forward
ardently to Rome, no longer backward to dead Troy. These two
books thus conclude the tale of Aeneas' weary travels; we may
discuss later the extent to which they belong to a second "tetrad."

I Book Five

Framed by sequences describing the arrival in (1–41) and de-
parture from (762–871) Sicily, Book Five concentrates on two events
that occurred in close order after the Trojans landed at Drepanum:
first, the holidaylike atmosphere of the anniversary games commemo-
rating dead Anchises (42–603), and second, the near-tragic results
of Juno's attempt to destroy the Trojan fleet once again, this time
by fire (604–761). The frame is made clear not only by the opposite
movements of arrival and departure but also by the repeated motifs
involving Palinurus, Aeneas' pilot, Neptune, and nautical dangers.
The four parts, arrival, initial happiness, disaster caused by hostile
deities, and departure repeat the standard rhythm employed con-
sistently by Vergil to set forth the frustrating wanderings of the
homeless Trojans.[1]

More than half of Book Five focuses on the commemorative
celebrations in honor of Anchises. Since Vergil did not elaborate
the details of Anchises' funeral in Book Three, at the time of the
death, and since these celebrations mark an exact year from the
date of death, it is easy to think of these as the funeral rites, and
Vergil no doubt encourages the illusion. To enhance his purpose he
exploits a well-known Homeric parallel, for in general structure and
in specific detail the games held by Aeneas for Anchises recall the
games which Achilles in *Iliad,* Book Twenty-three, held to honor
dead Patroclus, Patroclus who had died a few days previously and
just received a lordly funeral.[2] As always, however, Vergil's use of
familiar Homeric situations is suggestive in manifold ways. If, on
the one hand, we entertain the illusion that these are indeed
funeral games, on the other hand we cannot help contrasting the
moods of Aeneas and Achilles. Achilles had been, as he well knew,
responsible for his friend's death, and he remained inconsolable
amid the festivities in which the rest of the Greeks noisily partici-
pated; he was a figure apart, tragic, smouldering with an unhappi-
ness that contrasted with the prevailing gay excitement. Aeneas has
had nothing to do with Anchises' death; it was, as he exclaimed in

Book Three, an unforeseen disaster which seemed at the time the ultimate misfortune he could bear. Moreover, the year's interval since the death has permitted him to overcome his sorrow; he can participate fully in the pleasures of the contestants, without guilt or latent grief for the dead. Patroclus had died in combat, and the war setting inevitably affects the games of the *Iliad*; we can look forward beyond Book Twenty-three to the destruction of Troy and to the death of Achilles that shortly precedes the Greek victory, and so the funeral games for Patroclus prefigure those held in honor of Achilles himself. In Sicily, however, war seems like a dim memory of the distant past; certainly Anchises did not fall in battle. And yet Vergil has an eye on the future: each of the games anticipates general circumstances of war, glancing at the behavior that makes for victory or defeat, and quite evidently the footrace involving Nisus and Euryalus prefigures the tragic wartime mission in which the two will meet their death in Book Nine. So warfare does not weigh heavy on the Trojans in Sicily, but Vergil and we do view these happy contests in the light of the bloody contests which will repeat their basic motifs. Other significant parallels or contrasts could no doubt be noted, but I shall limit myself to one final ironic point. Although Aeneas has not caused Anchises' death, which occurred a year ago, he has caused the death of Dido within the past few days. Taking our cue from Achilles' situation, we are perhaps expected to imagine how Aeneas might have honored Dido, dead through his implicit guilt, had his destiny permitted him to know of her death and to be present at her funeral. Vergil makes sure that memories of Dido do intrude upon these happy contests.[3]

Two themes characterize the Vergilian treatment of all four contests: (1) an ethical rather than realistic account of victory; (2) an accent on the note of vicarious sacrifice in the context of every success. In the ship race, the rounding of the outer marker provides the opportunity for a lesson on moderation: the ship of Gyas, which goes too cautiously and too widely around, allows Cloanthus room to go between him and the rock and so forge into the lead and eventually gain victory; the ship of Sergestus, which goes too close to the rock, scrapes on it, losing all its oars on the inside—and meanwhile Mnestheus skims around on the outside and hotly pursues Cloanthus. There is then a second sequence to explain why Cloanthus defeats Mnestheus, for each of them has steered his ship intelligently. But Cloanthus prays to the sea deities, who then speed him toward the finish. Thus the two clever captains are separated; and the two inferior captains are distinguished in the different results of caution—mere delay—and rashness. Cloanthus gets his victory, but he must pay to the gods in return the white bull that he vowed (235 ff.).[4] This vicarious sacrifice is, however, considerably less dramatic than the "sacrifice" of Gyas' pilot Menoetes. Blaming Menoetes for his excessive caution, Gyas angrily picked him up and threw him overboard. The result, in this artificial holiday setting, is of course comic (see 181). Gyas merely increases the confusion aboard his ship and so enables Mnestheus to pass him also; as for Menoetes, he returns sputtering to the surface and clambers up on the unlucky rock to await rescue. At the end of the book, however, Palinurus will be violently hurled overboard by a divine force, a sacrificial victim devoted to the inexplicable demands of the gods, and this time there will be only tragedy: death for the pilot, laments for Aeneas.

From the shore the Trojans move to a grassy natural stadium, where Aeneas sets the second contest, a footrace (286 ff.). As the race nears the finish, five runners are packed closely together in the following order: Nisus, Salius, Euryalus, Elymus, and Diores. Suddenly Nisus has the misfortune to slip in a pool of blood from a sacrificed bull. Realizing that he has no chance, he acts instantaneously to insure victory for his friend Euryalus by tripping up Salius. Thus Euryalus, Elymus, and Diores come in first, second, and third and take the prizes. When Salius quite rightly protests the foul committed against him, he gets a special prize; and then Nisus is compensated for his bad luck. Euryalus wins, however, because of Nisus' sacrifice, a willing act of friendship. The pool of blood here serves an immediately comic end, but its symbolic value extends beyond to the tragic sacrifice of Palinurus and Nisus' later self-sacrifice in combat for his beloved Euryalus.[5]

The third contest matches two boxers, the eager and confident young Trojan Dares against the reluctant and aging Sicilian Entellus. As we would hope, the confident boaster loses when Entellus, aroused to anger after a slow start, prevails on the basis of greater ability and, presumably, experience. It is a highly ethical account of victory.[6] At the end it is necessary for Aeneas to intervene so as to save Dares from fatal injury. Alone in the arena, Entellus demonstrates what would have happened to Dares: he brings his right hand, encased in the boxing *caestus,* down on the skull of his prize, a bullock, and shatters it. The poor animal replaces Dares (476).

In the final contest four archers compete to hit a dove which is tied by the leg to a pole and flutters desperately to gain its freedom.

Hippocoön hits the pole right below the dove; Mnestheus hits the cord holding the bird; as it flies for freedom, Eurytion pierces it, after invoking the spirit of his dead brother; and Acestes, with nothing left to aim at, shoots his arrow straight up into the air and sees it miraculously turn into flames. The progression is obvious, and Acestes wins.[7] The dove, the innocent target of the arrows, like the bull of Entellus, serves as a vicarious victim.

The games continue now with a display of horsemanship by the young Trojans led by Ascanius (545 ff.), and more pleasures might have been in store for the spectators if Fortune had not suddenly changed (604). Some or most of the women, indifferent to the athletics of the men and unable to enjoy them, have been walking disconsolately along the shore, sharing their miseries and sense of alienation from the promised future, when Juno seizes her opportunity and sends Iris down to fire the women into violent action. The ships continue to be her target, but now what was a metaphorical fire of irrationality inside Juno manifests itself as her weapon of attack. When the smoke rises from the fleet, Ascanius spurs his horse to the scene and frightens the women away. Then Aeneas comes up (*pius Aeneas*, 685) and prays anxiously for help, which comes in the form of a sudden downpour that extinguishes the fire. Four ships are totally ruined; the remainder can be restored to service quickly. In this situation Aeneas shows little decision. Elderly Nautes, a "father substitute," offers good advice (709 ff.), and when Aeneas still remains uncertain, Anchises himself appears in a dream (722 ff.). The outcome of it all is that the original advice is followed: accepting the loss of the ships, Aeneas picks out the young and middle-aged to continue on with him to Italy, leaving the elderly and the larger part of the women in a settlement to be governed by Acestes. It is a repetition of what happened at their departure from Crete (see 3.190), but also the loss of the women will enable the Trojans to unite later with the Italians in their new "home."

When they sail from Sicily their feelings are far from happy, divided as they are by their sense of lost friends and their uncertain hopes for the future. Venus intervenes on their behalf with Neptune, who promises to guarantee them a safe passage on the overnight trip to Cumae. His price is "one head," that of Palinurus. Aeneas falls asleep happily (828)—he will awake with groans (869) —and in the meantime the god claims his victim. There is no logical explanation for the cruel way Sleep works to deceive the conscientious pilot, then resorts to violence; Vergil did not try to account for it. That is the unfair part of life, and he merely registered it, connecting it with his familiar theme about the price paid to build Rome. In 6.347 ff., Palinurus offers another account of his death based on his limited human knowledge, but here we see differently. The book ends on a bitter note.

II BOOK SIX

Two lines at the opening of Book Six effect the transition from the tearful apostrophe to Palinurus in Five to the somber arrival at Cumae, a small harbor surmounted by a strongly fortified hill or acropolis several miles north of modern Naples. Similarly, two lines at the end of the book will record the departure from Cumae and the short sail north along the coast to Caieta (modern Gaeta). Within that frame of arrival and departure, Aeneas fulfills the two missions which have been assigned him at different times: first, he consults the Sibyl about his immediate future in Italy, as Helenus directed him to do (see 3.441 ff.); secondly, he contrives to enter the underworld by an opening near the sea, a cave on the shores of Lake Avernus, and there succeeds in meeting his father, precisely as Anchises had urged in the important dream appearance in Sicily (see 5.731 ff.). The uniting factor in these two separate adventures is the Sibyl, for she alone advises Aeneas how to gain entrance into the underworld and guides him the perilous way to Anchises.

While the Trojan crew light a fire and look around for food, Aeneas climbs up the citadel to the cave of the Sibyl. (Even today the cave can be visited, and it produces almost as much awe without the Sibyl as Vergil assigns it with its venerable occupant.) Instead of staging an immediate encounter between Trojan and seer, Vergil imposes a delay by repeating a motif we have seen effectively employed in Book One: he places Aeneas before a set of reliefs or paintings, viewed on the two doors of the shrine, and describes these works of art which the Trojan studies as he awaits the Sibyl. So in Book One Aeneas studied scenes of the Trojan War represented on Juno's temple while awaiting Dido. There the pictures bore directly on Aeneas: they moved him to tears, he drew inferences about the humanity of the Carthaginians, and the final picture of Penthesilea prefigured—in a way that we, not he, could feel—the tragic fate of Dido. No such obvious connection exists at Cumae between viewer and scenes, and yet there are several tantalizing details which encourage one to pursue the search for relevance. Daedalus, once he escaped from Cretan pursuit here, erected this shrine to Apollo and recorded on the door panels his adventures in Crete and during his escape. Aeneas has also escaped from Greek pursuit, and he is a devotee of Apollo. Daedalus has represented Crete; Pasiphae's monstrous love for the bull; the foul offspring of their union, the Minotaur; and the coming of Theseus from Athens to kill this monster; the famous labyrinth; and the way Theseus escaped by exploiting the passion felt by Ariadne for him. Aeneas has never literally faced a Minotaur, and yet he has been in a spiritual labyrinth fighting his own psychological monsters; his wanderings since Troy can be characterized by that phrase used by Vergil to describe the Cretan maze: *inextricabilis error* (27). Moreover, Theseus' cruel treatment of Ariadne, who helped him to end his "wanderings" and then was abandoned by him, constitutes a prototype of Aeneas' relation toward Dido.[8] Finally, the approaching trip into the underworld carries with it associations of wandering in a labyrinth.[9]

The Sibyl's sudden approach interrupts Aeneas' reveries. Escorting him into her cave, she almost immediately falls into a prophetic frenzy, and Aeneas pleads through her to Apollo for a clear set of directions about his settlement in Italy. The answer (83 ff.) is far from clear or encouraging. It emphasizes nothing but war, which it sets forth paradoxically in terms of the horrible experiences suffered by Aeneas at Troy. He has another Trojan War, it seems, to endure in Italy; the names of places and combatants alone will be new, but the pattern will recur: another futile war because a Trojan takes a foreign bride and so stirs an army against his people, an army that will boast a counterpart of formidable Achilles. There is a way out of this tragic conflict, so paradoxical as to seem for the moment incapable of realization. If Aeneas can secure help from a Greek city, the beginning has been made toward safety.

It is plain that Vergil has chosen this strategic moment to remind us, as well as Aeneas, of a key pattern for the second half of the epic. Aeneas bravely accepts the inevitable and never seems to allude to the pattern in later books. In fact, his attitude changes so radically as the result of his encounter with Anchises in Elysium that we can safely say that he is liberated from his Trojan nightmares; he does *not* think of the Italian war as another Trojan War. We might call it a war of unwilling conquest, forced upon Aeneas by the irrational, uncontrolled hostility of Turnus and the others who openly disobey their king and frustrate his pacific intentions. If so, then Aeneas is right in living in the present for the future, and those people are wrong who insist on rigidly asserting the parallels between Trojans now and the guilty Trojans of Paris' time, between heroic Greeks with their righteously indignant Menelaus, his brother Agamemnon, the great Thessalian prince Achilles and, on the other hand, the Italian leader(s) and the strangely warped reasons that have propelled them into this carnage. Aeneas is *not* Paris or Hector; that becomes obvious as soon as Vergil describes his betrothal with the "foreign bride" Lavinia in Book Seven. The Italian hero Turnus is *not* Menelaus or Achilles, as he and the Sibyl suggest. And yet Vergil does utilize the Homeric pattern to make some crucial implications about this war. In a certain sense, Aeneas does go through another "Trojan War" and Books Seven through Twelve do parallel the *Iliad,* but in them Aeneas increasingly plays out the roles assigned by Homer to his Greeks, and the Italians seem to take upon them the part of Homer's Trojans. At the end, then, when Aeneas kills Turnus, we are expected to recall how Homer portrayed the killing of Hector by Achilles: Turnus has become the noble but inadequate Trojan whose death signifies the effective collapse of Trojan resistance, and Aeneas has become that insuperable warrior and tragic figure Achilles, whose victory means much to others, but comes too late to spare him from misery.[10]

Aeneas quickly swallows his disappointment, then turns the subject to his need to visit Anchises (106 ff.). He reminds the Sibyl that he has heroic prototypes who went to the underworld and returned: Orpheus, Pollux, Theseus, and Hercules. The most apposite parallel he ignores, both because he could not know of it by himself and because it is so obvious to Vergil's audience that it need not be mentioned. Vergil is of course following in the path of Homer and developing a motif used in *Odyssey,* Book Eleven. I say "developing," for Vergil moves with great poetic originality, just as, nearly 1350 years later, Dante, who took the Roman as his guide for *Inferno,* developed the general pagan scheme of the underworld in a powerful new way appropriate to his age and genius. Odysseus did not enter the underworld, but visited the Shades, who spoke to him on the confines of their abode; he observed things without deeply experiencing them, and Homer did not locate Elysium near the Shades or require a national parade of coming Ithacans. Vergil builds his whole account toward the climax of the future Romans parading before Aeneas and so inspiring him with a passionate longing to promote that future. But throughout his trip among the dead, Aeneas encounters people who profoundly move his emotions; he sympathizes with them and must be torn from them by action of the Sibyl.

Entrance to the underworld is not an automatic thing, even for a hero of Aeneas' stature. First he must perform two acts: he must find the mysterious "golden bough" and bury a comrade Misenus, who drowned while Aeneas was consulting the Sibyl. Both of these acts are ritually significant. Misenus seems to function, like Palinurus, as a vicarious victim to the gods; his magnificent funeral helps to placate the deities of death, who then permit living Aeneas to visit their realm and escape. Even more symbolically important is the golden bough, which Frazer found so fascinating that he chose it as the title for his lengthy study of anthropological material—Greek, Roman, and other—concerning death and resurrection, replacement, and succession. Vergil uses it to suggest the ambiguous condition of Aeneas in the underworld, a glitter of gold in the darkness, heroic vitality and corporeality among twittering spirits, purposefulness and hope in a climate of defeated purposes, of frustrated or at least ended hopes.[11] While collecting wood for Misenus' pyre, Aeneas is guided by Venus' doves to the tree with its special bough. Accordingly, having celebrated the funeral and performed solemn sacrifice of black animals to the gods of the dark underworld, he grasps the bough and bravely steps into the cave by Avernus, following the Sibyl on the dark eery route to Anchises.

Anchises had implied in the dream that Aeneas would do nothing but speak with him. In fact, there are many preliminary encounters and experiences for the Trojan, which add up to a poetic explanation of life, its rewards and punishments; this "explanation" helps to explain Aeneas better to himself and us. For although his basic humanity inclines him to feel attached to each of the figures singled out by Vergil for elaboration in the various regions of the underworld, he and we perceive that he does not belong with them, that his true place is indeed with his father in Elysium, among the future Romans. So the journey through the preliminary stages before Elysium serves a didactic and a protreptic purpose. When Aeneas parts in turn from Palinurus, Dido, and Deiphobus and passes Tartarus without personally experiencing it, he frees himself implicitly from old faults and ties to move eagerly into the domain of light and happiness where Anchises reveals to him his true purpose.

The darkness of all the regions visited by Aeneas before Elysium emerges emphatically from the start: it seems to him that his path is like one that winds its way through black woods on a dark, largely moonless night, and everything he dimly sees appears menacing. This blackness, to be contrasted so sharply with the sunny, colorful Elysium, suggests the essential character of this region, its negativity, lack of achievement, deep regret, hopelessness. Vergil develops his account of the underworld largely through dramatic encounters between Aeneas and the spirits of people he once knew. First, then, at the shores of the underground Acheron, he meets Palinurus.

Palinurus was an innocent victim of circumstances, sacrificed to the demands of Neptune. In his life of adequate service as Aeneas' helmsman and in his premature death, Palinurus epitomizes the sad fates of many human beings. Moreover, since he perished far from his friends, he did not receive burial, and so he finds himself in worse misery below. Unless someone buries his corpse, he must remain by the shores for a hundred years, unable to reach his ultimate place in the underworld. He tries to affect his cruel fate by making a personal appeal to Aeneas to get him across the Styx. Even though the poem says nothing, we may reasonably assume that Aeneas was deeply moved and wanted to help; the Sibyl intervenes and prevents any sympathetic comment from Aeneas. In the future the gods will compensate Palinurus somewhat by terrorizing the peoples of Italy near whom his body lies untended, until they collect his bones and give him a funeral; and his name will be preserved at Cape Palinurum there. The drowned pilot and Aeneas, his former commander, must content themselves with that. Dead and living must now part. As Palinurus wretchedly watches, Aeneas boards Charon's ferry and vanishes across the Styx.

On the other side, Aeneas quickly moves past the monstrous watchdog Cerberus into a region defined by the judgment of Minos as the place for those who lived wretched lives. In one part lament the prematurely dead and men falsely condemned to death; in another are the suicides, who bitterly regret now their loss of life; and finally Aeneas sees the fields of mourning, where are wandering the women who ruined themselves for love. He receives a violent shock to discover that Dido moves among these women, seen hauntingly like a new moon in the dark night sky (453–54), and he speaks to her with tears of love and regret, trying once again to explain to her the reasons for his departure. She turns away bitterly, unmoved by his passionate words; Aeneas is compelled to experience the same hard, seemingly unfeeling stubbornness as he exhibited toward Dido at the time of his departure. As she walks away spurning him, he can only look after her with tears that epitomize his love and pity. Anyone who needs proof that Aeneas loved Dido can find it here; and here, too, is Vergil's final comment on Dido's irresponsible, self-destructive passion.

Next the Sibyl and Aeneas enter the fields crowded by famous warriors. Vergil lists many distinguished Homeric Greeks and fallen Trojans, then selects Deiphobus as a representative spokesman. Deiphobus also gives Aeneas a shock, not so much because his death is a surprise (like Dido's), but because the manner of his death has sent him to the underworld horribly disfigured. In this and other details Vergil implies that these famous warriors—men like Achilles, Patroclus, Sarpedon, and Hector are not here—have led a defective existence and now suffer for it. They committed themselves to warfare for wrong reasons—conquest, loot, vengeance—and when they fell their lives were without merit. Hence in the underworld their spirits go about clothed in useless armor and they display their "glorious" wounds, but it is all vanity. "Heroic" Deiphobus is one of the least honorable Trojans: he acquired Helen after Paris was killed, and she betrayed him on the last night to her Menelaus, who took the usual vengeance of outraged husband upon adulterer: he cut off nose and ears and, no doubt, genitals as well. Aeneas, being more than mere warrior, does not belong here, much as he wants to linger with poor Deiphobus.

As they hurry on, they pass the massive walls surrounding Tartarus, where people are punished for active sin—not, as in the places already described, for making messes of their own lives. They do not perpetuate unhappiness suffered on earth, for many of them enjoyed their crimes while alive. So in Tartarus they are tortured in various ways. Tartarus was an old Greek concept and *Odyssey*, Book Eleven, lists some of the archetypal sinners, like Tantalus, with their punishments. Vergil, however, adds to the conventional denizens of this place people whom the Roman morality would gravely condemn: those who have participated in civil war, traitors, violators of the sacred blood bonds of *pietas* and the bonds of clientship (608 ff.). Aeneas does not need to view their punishments; theirs are not his temptations, so it suffices for him to hear that such people are punished. He has suffered from such, for example Sinon.

Elysium also has its walls; here Aeneas leaves his golden bough, and here he enters a happy colorful, brightly illuminated region. After reviewing the general aspect of these sunlit meadows, Aeneas locates his father in a valley. Anchises is watching a group of souls as they prepare to return to life. It amazes Aeneas, after all his personal troubles, that anyone should be so insane as to want to live again (719–21). To answer Aeneas in part, Anchises produces a theory of metempsychosis based on traditional Greek speculation

(Pindar, Plato, and the Stoics). Then to convince Aeneas of the desirability of reliving, the father explains the coming achievements of particular returning souls who, as Aeneas' descendants, will advance Rome to its extraordinary heights. It is significant that Anchises' lesson works and that Aeneas, after this symbolic "death" in the underworld, does return to life passionately dedicated to the future.

The parade of great Romans receives careful organization. First Aeneas sees his direct descendants, the kings of Alba Longa (founded by his son) as far as Romulus, who will of course found Rome (760–80). Romulus suggests to Vergil the refounder of Rome after the civil wars, Augustus, and so he glances forward quickly to the end of the series in his own day, to the ultimate justification of Aeneas' efforts. He had done the same thing in Jupiter's predictions in Book One. There is another reason for placing Augustus here in the center of the parade, for although he did fulfill much of Romulus' role, Augustus would not have wished to be called a king like Romulus; on the other hand, he was not really a Republican senator or "first man" of the country. By placing him in the center, Vergil suggests that he is a blend of these two Roman traditions, fulfilling the best of both. The remainder of the parade, then, consists of Republican heroes from Brutus, who ended the monarchy in 509 B.C., the great generals and leaders of the third and second centuries, to young Marcellus, Augustus' nephew recently dead in 23 B.C. From all these Anchises draws the lesson that the Roman exists to rule strongly and justly, to conquer, be merciful, and establish firm, fair peace. Art is for others, Vergil modestly asserts (847).

The cumulative effect of this Roman parade is dynamic: Aeneas is fired with love for the coming fame of his people (889). When he knows what his efforts will produce, the details of immediate wars and labor, which Anchises does not minimize (890–92), do not depress him. His return to the Trojan fleet is cast in highly ambiguous terms by Vergil, who has thereby caused a critical controversy which remains far from settled even now.[12] There are two gates of Sleep as possible exits from the underworld. The first, made of horn, is reserved for genuine shades; the second, made of ivory, is used to send false dreams to men. When Vergil says that Aeneas departed by the ivory gate (898), what does he mean? Nothing in particular except that Aeneas was not a shade? That it was all a false dream? That Aeneas is a false dream in pursuit of a falsehood of Roman greatness (a typical modern cynical view)? That the experience was a kind of dream, whose truth or falsehood ultimately depends upon Aeneas and his descendants? Whatever he meant, Vergil definitely sets us thinking as he returns Aeneas, more Roman than Trojan now, to the world of the awake and living.

✥ V ✥

WAR, A MONSTER OF TWO
FACES: BOOKS SEVEN AND EIGHT

Many people have an ambivalent attitude toward war: they hate
the suffering and destruction it causes, but they admire the peace
and political order it often brings in its train. Ruthless politicians
may choose a war of conquest only pausing to calculate the risk;
responsible politicians, knowing the two-faced monster better, never
enter war without a feeling of pain and guilt. The struggles of con-
science experienced by Woodrow Wilson are a case in point. The
Romans, too, for all their military successes, recognized war's am-
bivalence, especially after experiencing the effects of civil war for
nearly a century. In Book Six Vergil conveys this mixed attitude
of hate-love in his close juxtaposition of the selfless Republican
generals (Decii, Drusi, Torquatus, Camillus, 6.824–5) and the self-
seeking dynasts Caesar and Pompey. Anchises tries to set rational
limits on war (6.851–53) so as to make it exclusively beneficial.
However, when Aeneas stands over wounded Turnus in Book
Twelve, as we shall see, the very words of Anchises seem to be in
conflict; in any case, the rational action is not easily discerned, or
when noted, chosen under the pressure of combat.

Books Seven and Eight record the first stages of war in Italy. In
Book Seven war is unequivocally a monster of destruction: all the
negative symbols which have been so brilliantly employed earlier
in Books Two and Four now belong to it. In Book Eight, on the
other hand, Vergil shows war's other face to Aeneas and us: it be-
comes a necessary evil leading to a greater good. Before Aeneas,
Hercules came to the site of Rome and resorted to "creative vio-
lence" so as to free the people from the monster Cacus. After
Aeneas, in the scene depicted on his new shield, Augustus will fight
the battle of Actium and, by defeating Antony, Cleopatra, and their
monstrous Oriental forces, will establish an orderly, creative peace.
Much as Aeneas hates war, after experiencing its destructiveness and
futility at Troy, he is destined to act as the link between Hercules
and Augustus. His war will make Rome possible.

63

Those who analyze the *Aeneid* as a "trilogy" argue that Books Five through Eight form a unit essentially about Rome. Are these four books really so integrated with each other, so elegantly interconnected as Books One through Four? I do not think so. Whereas Books One and Four, containing the Dido story, form a frame for the narrative of past events which Aeneas provides in Two and Three, and present and past crucially combine to affect Dido's feelings and ultimate tragedy, few would claim that Books Five and Eight or Six and Seven show similar structures. Vergil's interest in Rome produces, of course, connections between Six and Eight. However, Book Five fits with difficulty into a trilogy scheme, and Book Six seems far more patently designed to end a development (Aeneas' *Odyssey*) and Book Seven to initiate a new development (his *Iliad*). In this respect, we should remember that Vergil carefully introduces us in Book Seven to Turnus, equipping him with all his essential thematic qualities; consequently, the third portion of the supposed "trilogy," which has been christened The Tragedy of Turnus, loses some of its integrity to this unlikely "unit" of Books Five through Eight. Except for Books One through Four, then, it proves awkward to apply the theory of the *Aeneid* trilogy: the tripartite groups cannot be isolated without considerable distortion.

I BOOK SEVEN

Circumstances in Italy strongly favor Aeneas upon his arrival. It seems indeed like a fairy tale: an elderly king has an only child, a daughter who is just now at the right age for marriage; many suitors have flocked to the court to woo her, but every one has been rejected because of a series of portents surrounding the princess. A swarm of bees has occupied a sacred laurel tree dedicated to Apollo in the center of the palace (59 ff.). While sacrificing, the princess has suddenly been engulfed in flames without harm (71 ff.). What the priests predicted in interpreting these omens has been supported by a dream of Latinus: a foreigner must marry the princess, and the union will result in great glory for Latinus' descendants. There is, of course, a negative note which receives little emphasis now, but does underlie the Italian eagerness for war: the swarm of bees in the palace betokens a foreign army taking power in Latinus' city; the fire around the princess signifies glory for her, but destructive war for her people. Even if destiny favors the marriage of Aeneas and princess, the likely victims of such a union may oppose it. Rumor is operating among the Italians, presumably with all her typical malevolence, at the time of the Trojan arrival. And it is probably significant that Vergil uses the phrase *Laomedontia pubes* here (105) to identify the Trojans, for Laomedon is the most *ignoble* of the Trojan kings, archetype of deception and impiety. It is as though the phrase connotes Italian suspicion of the foreigners from the beginning.

The first moments on land increase Aeneas' happiness. As in Africa, he sits down to a humble meal with his men, this time even without meat. Not having regular plates, they make some of *pasta*, and when they have eaten the wild fruit picked near the shore, it is only natural for them to satisfy their hunger by eating the "plates" or "tables" under this food. Innocent Ascanius jokingly comments on the fact with the very words—"we are eating our tables"—which echo the frightening prediction of the Harpy (3.125).[1] With this easy escape from the menace, all is gaiety (130,147) and confident activity. The next day, Aeneas has the region explored, sends picked men to make peaceful arrangements with the king, and starts the walls of a modest camp near the shore.

If this landing reminds us somewhat of the arrival in Africa, the details of negotiations with Latinus provide an even closer parallel.[2] Like Carthage, the city is flourishing and alive with youthful activity. The ambassadors press toward a temple which, like Juno's temple in Carthage, serves as a center for political activity. As at Carthage, Ilioneus is spokesman for the Trojans. He speaks of the greatness of Aeneas, their peaceful purposes, and makes a modest request of the king, who, with the same generosity as Dido earlier, offers more than they asked. The reason for these parallels is not clear yet, for the pattern has not been fully developed. There is another interesting note that needs emphasis. Vergil describes the temple where Latinus greets the Trojans as an "august building," a "senate house" (170, 174), patently using terms from Roman politics. He may be suggesting only that these Latins possess institutions which will easily combine with the Trojan ways to produce Roman practices; or he may be implying that already before Aeneas there are "Roman institutions" in Italy which the Trojans desperately need. If so, can the Trojans really bring improvement? What exactly does Aeneas have to offer to the Italians? Despite all the talk about Dardanus, by Ilioneus and Latinus, it appears undeniable that the Trojans, wretched "exiles" that they are, receive from Latinus far more than they can repay.

Any situation of happiness among Trojans provokes the opposite sentiment in Juno, who then attempts to disrupt it, using some intermediary and any of her characteristic means of creating disorder. The happy departure from Sicily in Book One was ruined by her storm; the happy return to Sicily and imminent second departure was marred by the burning of the fleet in Book Five. Now she starts again, acting in ways that specifically recall her irrational destructiveness in 1.33 ff. After a brief metaphorical description of Juno's anger (291), Vergil assigns her a wild soliloquy, complete with impertinent comparisons with other deities' vengeance, that spurs her into action. She approaches the Fury Allecto, "prays" to her for help in upsetting peace between Latinus and Aeneas, and then lets Allecto use her typical devices, snakes and fire, to bring on a war. The war can be compared to the effects of a storm (586 ff.), just as Juno's storm in Book One contained overtones of warfare. Thus the parallel with the details and the symbolism of Book One is important for Vergil. One thing, however, is not parallel: the basic sequence is reversed. Instead of having the disturbance of Juno followed by happy arrival, Vergil here starts with happy arrival and then depicts Juno disturbing it. Implicitly, then, the parallel has been adduced mainly to emphasize the nonparallel arrangement, for the confusion caused by Juno here at the beginning of Seven receives no check from a god like Neptune. The efforts of a good man Galaesus, which resemble those of the just senator in the Neptune simile (1.148 ff.), have the ironic result of causing his death. What is going to stop Juno this time? is our question.

Another parallel of a different type occurs in Juno's wild speech (319 ff.). Resorting to details of the Trojan war, the goddess calls Aeneas a second Paris, his marriage the cause of ruin for his second Troy. As I said earlier, Aeneas does *not* draw express parallels between events in Troy and in Italy. The Sibyl does in 6.86 ff., and thereafter only Aeneas' enemies affect to detect a resemblance between events. Juno here is the first to do so; Amata will invoke similarly invidious details (363); and in later books Turnus will do the same. In all cases, the context implies the fallacy of the comparison; as here, where Juno's irrationality is climaxed by the Trojan allusion. And when we press the details of the comparison, the error becomes manifest. Is Aeneas a "second Paris"? Of course not. He has never met the princess, who is neither married nor given the provocative beauty of Helen. He does not come, then, into an adulterous relation with another man's wife; he does not seduce her into leaving with him for his home. To put it frankly, Aeneas never does see Lavinia during the rest of the epic, never expresses any feelings for her or interest in her. All his erotic passions have been burned out in his two loves—Creusa at Troy and Dido at Carthage. Now, a middle-aged widower seeking to found a dynasty in Italy, he is anything but an irresponsible Paris. Although the war is in a sense caused by Aeneas' marriage with the princess—in fact, by the mere prospect of the marriage—the circumstances differ sharply, and what blame there is falls on the prejudiced Italians, not on *pius Aeneas* and his Trojans.

Allecto cleverly develops feelings toward war in three stages, working first on Amata, mother of the princess, secondly on Turnus, lover of the princess and leading warrior in Italy, thirdly on the average Italian by means of a petty incident which provokes bloodshed. Amata has not favored the project of Latinus to marry their daughter to Aeneas. As Vergil told us earlier (56–57), she supported the candidacy of Turnus—we later learn that she is his aunt—and now he adds that, instead of bowing to expediency and Latinus' sage decision, she reacts violently, "burning, cooked by passions and anger" (345). Already vulnerable, Amata falls an easy victim to Allecto's designs; or, to put it another way, Allecto serves to symbolize Amata's own destructive intentions. With Allecto's snake slithering through her heart, poisoning her feelings, Amata goes to Latinus and tries to dissuade him, using tears and the false Trojan analogy of Paris-Aeneas. When that fails, her frenzy takes control. Vergil describes her wild movements through the town with sympathy—he calls her *infelix* (376) as he did Dido—and an ironic simile (378 ff.). Boys, playing with the kind of top that is whipped into movement, are delighted at the resultant gyrations; Amata resembles the top in her frantic rushing about. But where do the boys fit into Amata's situation? Here we are forced to think of the malevolent "game" being "played" by Allecto; she has whipped Amata into movement, and now she stands back delighted with the effect she has produced. Amata now seizes Lavinia, rushes off with her to the woods, pretending that she is under the inspiration of Bacchus; soon other women, equally driven, "fired" by irrational fury (392), hurry off to join her. In the midst of this counterfeit Bacchic "inspiration," fury-whipped Amata appeals to the *pietas* of these other women to defy Latinus. Thus, when she leaves Amata, the Fury Allecto has produced a scene of *furor impius*, madness making a travesty of *pietas* with false Bacchic rites and irrational attachment to the queen (at the expense of higher duties to king and political order). Aeneas had hoped to escape from the irra-

tionality of women when he left behind the despairing, emotional
Trojans in Sicily; now, soon after reaching Italy, he has become the
victim of other irrational women.

Allecto flies to Ardea (407 ff.), a few miles away, arriving in the
dead of night, symbolically appropriate to her black purposes. Her
victim, Turnus, does not fall so easily as Amata, for he exerts
some control over his passions. In fact, Vergil obscures the exact
situation, so that at first sight one gains the impression that Turnus
is drawn involuntarily into the war. Doesn't Turnus scorn Allecto's
use of persuasion? Can we not compare his self-controlled rejection
of her emotional arguments with the weak assent of Dido to the
blandishments of Anna, or of the Trojan women to Iris masquerad-
ing as Beroe (5.643)? Isn't Allecto then compelled to resort to force,
the use of the implanted torch? All these questions may be answered
in the affirmative without limiting Vergil's intention. Dido, we
remember, was treated both as a pathetic victim of a malevolent
Venus (operating with fire, pest, etc.) and as a guilty human being
capable of responsible action. Just as Venus can at times be regarded
as a symbol of Dido's human vulnerability to passion, maternal
affection, and other soft aspects of amatory sentiment, so Allecto
can symbolize the latent irrationality of Turnus. Turnus' noble dis-
missal of disguised Allecto occurred in his sleep, and similarly the
implanted torch came during sleep. Both might be subconscious
instincts, but the torch of irrationality becomes dominant. In any
case, once Turnus rises from that sleep, he never hesitates again
until Aeneas wounds him at the end of Book Twelve: he is the
incarnation of *furor* among the men. Soon he has a following among
the Rutulian males, and their slogan is: "Drive the enemy from
our territory and protect Italy!" (469)

It remains for Allecto to instill *furor* in the average Italians.
This she accomplishes with a diabolically ingenious *casus belli*—
like many such incidents fundamentally trivial in nature, yet ca-
pable of generating tremendous passion. Ascanius, in his boyish
enthusiasm as a hunter, shoots an arrow and wounds what, un-
known to him, is the pet deer of an Italian farmer named Tyrrhus.
Vergil, we can see, has taken one of his favorite symbols from Book
Four (the hunter unwittingly striking the deer) and made it live as
a real incident. Since we can hardly blame Ascanius (for Vergil
does not), we cannot approve of the violent reaction of the Italians,
who, instead of asking financial recompense for what after all is
only an animal (not even definitely dead), rush to arms. And yet
Ascanius' hunting reminds us of Aeneas' literal and figurative

hunting in Carthage, enough so that we can attribute to the Italians a sense of resentment against the Trojan interlopers and their careless treatment of private property, of native rights. In the resulting riot, Tyrrhus' eldest son dies of an arrow wound, and the Italian Galaesus, while attempting to stop the mob violence, is also slain. Who, we might wonder, killed him, an Italian or a Trojan? Vergil does not say, merely noting that he stood between the two motley bands (536). No Trojan dead are mentioned.

Allecto has done her work well, and Juno can easily finish it. In reverse order from their original involvement, the three groups arrive (573 ff.) to demand war of king Latinus. Vergil expressly comments on the irrationality and impiety of this demand (583–84), then focuses ironically on the king. Though fully aware that war is wrong, Latinus is too old and weak-willed to be able to act the part of the ideal king. He does not accept popular demands, but he yields by vacating his authority, leaving it to Turnus and other would-be leaders to assume responsibility. The simile of the unmoved cliff, followed by the collapse of Latinus and by the ship metaphors (586 ff.), might remind us of the storm of Book One and its symbolism: the ship of state here has become the prey of violent storms of revolution or civil chaos, and Latinus, the designated pilot, has forsaken his post.

To put the war in unmistakable perspective, Vergil evokes a familiar Roman ritual: the formal declaration of the "just war." The Latins, he asserts, had a practice which the Romans still respect today when Augustus declares war on Rome's foreign enemies in distant lands. The king—later the consul—would solemnly open the gates of the Temple of War, supported by the sober judgment of the assembled Fathers, and war would commence, to be waged rationally and bravely. This war is not, however, a "just war"; it is the product of tears, "snakes," "fire," a wounded pet deer, Allecto, savage Juno—in short, unreason or, in more thematic terms, *Furor impius*. The Trojans are not the foreigners they seem, for they have returned to their motherland and, after this insensate conflict, will be amalgamated with the Italians as "brothers." This war, then, is a prototype of the civil war which Aeneas' descendant Augustus alone could end. When Latinus refuses to perform the king's part, to open the doors when he knows it to be an impious act, Juno intervenes. She violently shatters the bolts of the doors, smashing them open; an act which epitomizes the whole character of the coming war. We have only to think of the apocalyptic vision granted to Venus and us by Jupiter in 1.293 ff. to realize what Vergil has done: he has shown the unwarranted release of savage *Furor impius*. Again he has taken an earlier symbol and dramatized it in action. Before the ideal of Rome can be achieved, these doors of war must be firmly shut. Can Aeneas do it, or does Italy await an even greater man?

With this final travesty of the hopes symbolically defined in Book One, with this ironic realization in action of the very reverse of the symbol, Vergil abandons his allusions to that book and now briefly reminds us of Homer and traditional war epics. It is time for an epic catalogue of the warring heroes (641 ff.). Of this section, I have room to say but a few things. Vergil speaks only of the Italians, emphasizing their ancient traditions, their links to heroes of Greek legend, their variety, and their basic strength. In mentioning Greek connections, however, the poet seems also to remind us of the Sibyl's prophecy. The Greeks take the Italians' side against the Trojans. Is this not a recurrence of the Trojan War? How will Aeneas ever find the support from a "Greek city" which he needs to break the horrible pattern? Finally we should note the dramatic way the catalogue opens and closes. Mezentius, despiser of the gods, is listed first, as if to summarize the impious madness of the Italians (647 ff.). Turnus and Camilla end the list—Turnus with emblematic armor defining the violence and pathos of his cause, Camilla as a women among the men automatically suggesting defeat (like Dido and her prototype Penthesilea in 1.490 ff.).[3] The pattern of defeat claims these three one by one: Mezentius in Book Ten, Camilla in Eleven, and finally Turnus in Twelve.

II BOOK EIGHT

The action of Book Eight takes place essentially in the space of three nights and days. During the first night and day (1–80), Aeneas decides to look for reinforcements for this war which he has not desired; a dream appearance of the Tiber god advises him to sail up the river to Evander's village (the site of later Rome). During the second night, he makes the short voyage and lands in the village at noon to share in a holiday in honor of its heroic benefactor Hercules (81–368). The third night and day (369–731) begin with an interlude among the gods, wherein Venus persuades Vulcan to make new armor for her son. The next day Aeneas completes his profitable discussions with Evander, rides a short distance north to the Etruscan army, and there, at Caere, he receives the armor which Vulcan has produced for him—a technical and artistic masterpiece, containing stories of future Roman warfare arranged around a central scene that depicts Augustus' victory at Actium. Framed, so to speak, by the past deeds of Hercules and the future accomplishments of Augustus, Aeneas acquires special significance in his role as warrior.[4]

When Aeneas, obedient to divine advice, sails up the Tiber to Evander's village, he finds the people there totally engrossed in festivities honoring Hercules. Vergil has, of course, designed this setting in order to establish links between Hercules and Aeneas that bear upon the central themes of the epic. To explain clearly the significance of Hercules here, Vergil has Evander recount the heroic feat by which Hercules freed his Arcadians of the monster Cacus. The story does not belong with the original labors of the hero, but it became attached to it, and the Augustan writers refer to it frequently for its contemporary applications.[5] Vergil fully integrates it with his themes by careful selection of details and imagery. Taking the basic myth—the killing of an evil monster by mighty Hercules —he attaches to Cacus the familiar associations of disorder (bestiality, wild beast's lair, murders, and fire) and attributes to Hercules the positive force of overcoming this evil incarnate.[6]

There are some important features in this narrative which prefigure later episodes of the epic, as we might expect from the way Vergil sets about to link Aeneas and Hercules. Not only is Cacus another version of that monster of Disorder, *Furor impius*, but he also specifically anticipates Turnus' behavior. Later in Book Ten, when Aeneas joins battle, Pallas has the misfortune to encounter Turnus and fall his inevitable victim. For the remainder of the war, Aeneas tries to catch up with Turnus and punish him for that cheap victory. Like Cacus, in 223, Turnus flees faster than the wind (12.733). Like Hercules, Aeneas will blaze with fury (219 and 12.946). When we hear this myth in Book Eight, the fury of Hercules seems heroic and righteous anger appropriate to the man and the situation, and we feel no sympathy for Cacus when Hercules kills him. The forces of order have triumphed over those of disorder, making possible the happy development of Evander's village (aboriginal Rome). But when we watch the drama of Turnus' death in Book Twelve, we feel more involved, as Vergil has intended; and we are tempted to blame Aeneas for hot fury, without seeing this event in the perspective of Turnus' actions or his significance as the last incarnation of disorder. At one level of interpretation at least, Aeneas acts like Hercules: he kills the man of disorder and thus makes the Rome of the kings and the Republic possible.

After the story Aeneas listens to a hymn in honor of Hercules

(285 ff.), some of whose details add to the links between the two. Like Aeneas, Hercules has wandered far and wide, suffering a thousand toils because of the savage hatred of unjust Juno. Then Evander escorts his guest through the village, and Vergil seizes the opportunity to remind his Roman audience of the difference between this diminutive Rome and what will come to be—all, of course, because Aeneas advances the cause begun by Hercules. With a last look at what one day will be the busy Roman Forum, then only a cow pasture, Aeneas bows his head to enter a rude hut where Hercules also spent his night (362 ff.). The identity between heroes is almost complete.

Aeneas' need of help is alleviated the next day. It turns out that Evander himself can provide very little, for his village is tiny and it too stands in constant danger from its Latin neighbors (473 ff.). This suffices, nevertheless, to fulfill the prophecy of the Sibyl: it is help from a "Greek City." Additional allies are providentially available in the persons of the Etruscans. Their king, it appears, was the blasphemous Mezentius who led off the list of Italian warriors; he had dealt so harshly with his subjects at Caere that they expelled him and have dedicated themselves to his destruction. The only thing that has delayed their vengeance is an oracle to the effect that they must have a foreign leader (503). Aeneas is obviously the "foreign leader," just as he is marked out to be Latinus' "foreign son-in-law." Accepting this and omens sent by Venus, Aeneas grimly but confidently (537) faces the coming war.

The final portion of Book Eight concentrates on the armor which Vulcan has made Aeneas—and thereby on the larger significance of Aeneas' military task. We receive a full description of the shield, for it contains emblematic scenes of later Roman history. Various events of Roman legend form small panels around an impressive, more spacious central scene. The little panels start with the twins born of the war god Mars and suckled by his animal the wolf, continue through warlike exploits of the kings, then end with chosen events from Republican wars. I emphasize the restriction to warfare because this shield does not merely duplicate the parade of Romans seen by Aeneas and Anchises in Book Six; it confines itself to war because that is the issue here: how to make Aeneas part of the long tradition of noble Roman warriors, selfless patriots, not irrational and ambitious young men like Turnus. The center of the shield represents the Battle of Actium (671 ff.). Augustus stands high on the stern of his battleship (680), as Aeneas does in 10.261; flames seem to surround his head, denoting divine favor, as they appear on

Aeneas' head (10.270). Against him are marshaled the barbarian
forces of the East with their motley, monstrous gods supporting
them; Vergil singles out dog-headed Anubis as representative (698).
The implication is clear: Augustus and his Western forces work for
Order, and Cleopatra and her savage Oriental masses epitomize
Disorder. While Cleopatra and her traitorous Antony survive, Dis-
cord or Disorder can rage, striding about in torn robe attended by
the goddess of War flailing with her bloody whip (702–3). The
right use of military force by Augustus, fully in the tradition of
Aeneas' and his descendants' practices, at last results in a "war to
end war." After Actium, Augustus did in fact close the gates of war
and symbolically pen up impious Fury, exactly as Vergil indicated
in 1.293. In this central scene, then, Vergil sets Aeneas' Italian war
in perspective: Aeneas will crush impious Fury in Italy and so en-
able the growth of little Rome throughout the peninsula into the
Mediterranean world; Augustus will crush impious Fury in the
Mediterranean and so establish Roman rule and creative peace in
all significant parts of the known world. Rightly employed, war can
be an honorable instrument; a true Roman will never make it an
end.

A brief look back at Homer's *Iliad* can shed some light on Vergil's
achievement here. If we think of the supposed "*Iliad* pattern," we
should be struck by the fact that Aeneas has not been acting like
any of Homer's Trojans. That becomes more obvious in the next
pair of books, but even here his withdrawal from the war scene
and now the present of armor secured from Vulcan by his mother
cannot help suggesting the situation of Achilles. If we do compare
him with Achilles, though, we see that he is a special kind of
Achilles, not guilty or tragic in Achilles' way; and the difference
becomes more apparent through study of their respective divine
shields. Achilles carries scenes which represent the total spectrum
of life—war and peace, marriage and death, festivals and lawcases.
The exact connection with the Greek hero is not spelled out, but
at least we sense the tragic fact that Achilles is fated to lose all
these things by early death, further that he has even cut himself
off from the wider community by his own fatal anger before this
moment in *Iliad,* Book Eighteen. Vergil, by contrast, restricts his
subject matter to warfare, Roman wars. Moreover, he has set this
shield episode as the climax of a development in Book Eight:
Hercules, Aeneas, and Augustus all belong together thematically as
representatives of Order who resort to force only to curtail the
destructive, utterly negative results of Disorder. The shield is re-

lated pointedly to Aeneas' role in the epic, defining its positive aspects, ignoring any possible tragic factors. Therefore, the final words of the book stress the historical relation, unconscious though Aeneas must be of it, between shield and bearer: "though ignorant of events, Aeneas marvels and takes pleasure in the pictures as he lifts to his shoulder the glory and destiny of his descendants" (730–31). As he hoists the shield, we might well think back to the earlier tableau of hope in defeat when he picked up Anchises and led Ascanius by the hand from burning Troy.

⊰ VI ⊱

AMBIGUITIES IN DEFEAT AND
VICTORY: BOOKS NINE AND TEN

After concentrating on Aeneas, absent at the site of Rome and then riding north into Etruria, Vergil now returns to the scene of war. Books Nine and Ten describe battle. In Book Nine we watch combat incited by Turnus who, in the absence of Aeneas, undoubtedly dominates the scene. His heroic feats occupy the major portion of the book, but in the center of them, functioning as both parallel and contrast, appear the striking deeds of Nisus and Euryalus. It is obvious that neither Turnus nor the Trojans achieve decisive advantages. Despite his fiery leadership, Turnus suffers checks in both his attacks, first from Cybele, then from the overwhelming numbers of Trojans to whom he has rashly exposed himself alone. Nisus and Euryalus prove inadequate to their charge and fall before the enemy. Thus Book Nine studies the moral qualities leading to defeat and, implicitly, those requisite for victory. No Trojan like Nisus or Euryalus can win the war, and Turnus, unless he changes—which is unlikely—cannot lead his Italians to victory. It needs a greater man. In Book Ten, that man, Aeneas, arrives on the scene, and the battle inclines decisively and deservedly for him. Although Turnus does kill Pallas, his role in the rest of the book is minimized to avoiding Aeneas. To replace inadequate Turnus, Mezentius moves in, performs magnificent deeds, then is killed by Aeneas. It is the beginning of the end for the Italians. In his first day of hard combat, Aeneas has displayed the complex qualities—sanity, valor, strength, hot indignation, cruelty, pitilessness, compassion (not all, by any means, lovely virtues in isolation)—which are demanded of a victorious general.

I BOOK NINE

Vergil has constructed Book Nine to highlight Turnus—in no other book will Turnus be so successful—and has provided important comparative types in Nisus and Euryalus. To begin with

75

the beginning, Vergil carefully accounts for the start of combat in order to emphasize the unjust, Juno-inspired aspects of the war. As we saw in Book Seven, Allecto ignited the war spirit; then, when that monster had done her work and departed for hell, Juno released the monster war, breaking down the doors of the temple instead of permitting the formal ceremony to take place in due time. Of the counteraction of the Trojans Vergil says nothing in either Book Seven or Eight. Certain Italians fall victims in the riot; their slayers are unnamed. No catalogue of Trojan heroes implies their eagerness for war; no measures parallel to those of the Italians are taken in the Trojan camp. In fact, Aeneas departs, not willing to start combat, leaving express orders (as we later learn in 9.40) that his Trojans must only defend themselves if attacked and not sally out from their walls. This is a war sought by the Italians, and in Book Nine the point is stressed when Juno sends Iris to Turnus in order to take advantage of Aeneas' absence. We meet Juno again at the end of the book as she significantly accepts the inadequacy of her hero Turnus (802).

Unhesitantly Turnus springs to arms, marshals his forces, and starts across the plain toward the Trojan encampment by the sea. Vergil captures that moment of order before violence convulses the picture by comparing Turnus to the majestic Ganges or Nile— swollen, powerful, and quiet (30–31). That moment does not last. Since Aeneas has left strict orders not to emerge from the walls, the Trojans reluctantly remain on the defensive. Turnus prances up on horseback, his red plume waving in the air, seizes a spear and throws it dramatically toward the Trojans to symbolize the start of battle. Nothing happens. Furious, frustrated, Turnus now loses his serene majesty and behaves, as a new simile indicates, like a wolf that prowls around a sheep-pen, trying to find an entrance and satisfaction for his savage hunger (59–64). For lack of any other target, he turns his energy in the direction of the Trojan ships, drawn up unguarded on the shore, and fires them.

The episode has multiple importance. First of all, burning the ships, a repetition of the incident of Book Five, epitomizes the destructive, irrational purposes of Juno. Turnus was to attack the Trojan camp; he had to content himself with this act of violence and somehow represent it publicly as a triumph. Secondly, Turnus' use of fire here and elsewhere in Book Nine should remind us of the symbolic torch planted in his breast by Allecto: his purposes, like Juno's, are essentially ruinous, irrationally inflamed and inflammatory. Thirdly, Vergil has alluded here to a famous incident of the

Iliad: the burning of the ships. In the *Iliad,* Greek ships are burned by Hector; the deed was the most menacing accomplishment of the Trojan leader, yet proved abortive because of the grand resistance of Ajax. Thus Vergil suggests that this war does not follow the pattern of the Trojan war, or if it does, that the Italians play the part of the *Iliad*'s Trojans and Turnus is the doomed Hector.

To emphasize the folly of Turnus, Vergil produces a scene which has no analogue in Homer. No Ajax drives off Turnus and puts out the fire; the goddess Cybele herself intervenes directly by metamorphosing the ships into mermaids. Although Homer's realism may be more to our tastes and, not long after, Ovid parodied Vergil's scene in his irreverent *Metamorphoses,* Vergil has selected this episode carefully and handled it discreetly. The miraculous change of ships to mermaids constitutes the fulfillment of a prophecy. Now that the Trojans have no further need of ships, having arrived in their promised land, Cybele can recover her favorite trees (to be thought of as nymphs?) in a new, deathless form as mermaids. And this transformation of the ships obviously looks forward to the major transformation which is the basic theme of the epic, the change of defeated homeless Trojans into Romans. Once we know the true meaning of the miracle, Vergil shows us how the Italians regard it. All but Turnus are shocked, frightened (123); Turnus alone retains his confidence. But Vergil calls him rash (*audaci,* 126). In a long, wild speech he gives his misinterpretation: the Trojans have been deprived of their ships, hence of any opportunity of escape; they are now at the mercy of the overwhelming Italian forces. Not content with this, Turnus goes on to invoke the *"Iliad* equation," in his case for the first time. He claims that, like Menelaus, he has had his wife taken violently from him and so, like Menelaus, he wages this war to avenge himself on guilty Troy (136 ff.). He, however, does not need miraculous Vulcan-made armor like Achilles, and he will not let any Hector of theirs drag out the war for ten years; he and his Italians are superior to Homer's Greeks! Vergil has already undermined Turnus' false parallels: Aeneas did not rob him of his "wife"; Turnus is no Menelaus or Achilles, but is right now acting the role of Hector; it is Aeneas now who has Vulcan-made armor. In the miracle of Cybele and the tragic irony of Turnus' comments, Vergil has done much to develop his basic themes.

When combat stops on this note and Turnus commands his men, happy at their achievements (157), to take their posts in picket stations around the Trojans, it might seem that we are watching

Troy besieged again. In fact, the situation forms a closer parallel to events of the *Iliad* when the Trojans were enjoying a brief advantage over the Greeks during Achilles' retirement: under the leadership of Hector they blockaded the Greeks in their camp on the Aegean shore and stationed pickets around them all night. In *Iliad*, Book Ten, Vergil found a night episode which he adapted to his special purposes. The Homeric original (today usually thought to be the work of a poet less able than Homer) describes the volunteer reconnoitering expedition of Odysseus and Diomedes, their murderous movements among the sleeping Trojans, and their capture of the Trojan spy Dolon, whom they kill after making him provide them information. It is a straightforward narrative: the Greeks are successful while the Trojans are foiled in a similar effort. Vergil complicates the situation by depicting a youthful pair of untried men who volunteer like heroes, imitate the murderous actions of the Greek heroes, then fall victim to the Italians. It surely cannot be said that they resemble the craven, butchered Dolon. But their inexperience and death set them apart from Odysseus and Diomedes. If anything, they are grander than the two Greeks, and their death establishes them, for Vergil and us, as true Roman heroes.

Nisus, the elder of the two, raises the question which underlies the whole episode: Do gods inspire men with their eager, burning desires or does each man make a god of the wild passion inside him (184–85)? Vergil's answer, worked out in the next 250 lines, seems to be: Both. Nisus says that he wants to serve as the messenger to Aeneas solely for fame (195), not for any material reward; and Euryalus responds to that love of praise (197). However, in proposing the mission to the Trojan chiefs, Nisus adds a new goal: he will locate Aeneas and return laden with spoils, the slaughterer of many men (242). As the Homeric parallel illustrates, the new goal need not exclude or take priority over the original one, but the danger is that it might. And it does. Wild human passion thus defeats the god-inspired desire. With a special gilded sword from Ascanius, Euryalus sets out, and Nisus dons a lionskin, emblematically significant, given him by Mnestheus (306).

When they begin to move through the Italian positions en route toward Aeneas, the two find their enemies in drunken sleep. Seizing the opportunity, Nisus begins to slaughter (320 ff.). When he has slain ten defenseless men, Vergil pauses to look at him: he resembles a hungry lion rampaging in a sheep-pen, its mouth bloody as it crunches through the flesh of the helpless animals (339 ff.). An insane hunger (340) drives on the lion; is Nisus an insane beast, too? The simile reminds us all too closely of that attached to Turnus in 59 ff. Wild Italian and Trojan differ only in that Nisus has been able to break into the pen and glut his bloody desire. Euryalus is also prey to this bestialized human passion: *fired* to action, he *rages* among sleeping forms (342–43); he goes beyond Nisus in *hotly* pressing forward to loot (350). Realizing that his companion is impelled by excessive passion (354), Nisus calls a halt to the slaughter. Unable to control himself, Euryalus seizes certain gold ornaments and dons a prized, but all too noticeable, helmet belonging to Messapus. In the dim light the helmet betrays him to a cavalry troop (373). There is a wild, nightmarish chase through the woods—a grim reminder of the carefree race in Sicily—and Nisus, unimpeded, escapes, but Euryalus' plunder weighs him down and he is captured. Thus the human passion has prevented the fulfillment of the god-given goal; it remains for Nisus, repeating the self-sacrifice of Sicily, to ennoble their deaths and so reveal the vestiges of a divine spark.

Nisus and Euryalus did have a noble passion and a noble love of each other; it was presumably their youthful inexperience that led to the reckless slaughter and plundering of the Italians. In the remainder of the book Vergil shows how Turnus' recklessness nearly led to his death, at any rate ruined a special opportunity to damage the Trojans.[1] There are three episodes where Turnus demonstrates his savage prowess: in the destruction of an exposed wooden tower (530 ff.), at the gates where he kills the disobedient guards Pandarus and Bitias (672 ff.), and inside the camp where alone he terrorizes the Trojans for a while (756 ff.).

At the tower Turnus employs his characteristic weapon of destruction, a torch, to fire the wood. One of the defenders tries to leap out and run back to the Trojan fortifications. Turnus pursues and tears him down from the very walls, like an eagle swooping down on a swan or rabbit, like a wolf snatching a lamb from the pen (563 ff.). This initial success leads to boastful words from Numanus, a relative of Turnus by marriage; he talks with the same folly as Turnus, and his death at the hands of Ascanius undoubtedly prefigures that of Turnus later.

After Numanus' death has qualified the success at the tower— after all, the tower was not structurally related to the wall and so its destruction is not strategically important—attention moves to the gates. Pandarus and Bitias are stationed there to keep them shut. Relying vainly on their gigantic size, they disobey Aeneas' strict orders and open the gates, inviting the enemy in to fight. Turnus fells Bitias like a bolt of lightning that destroys a massive

stone piling in the sea (706 ff.), then rushes on against Pandarus,
whose head he splits in two (749 ff.). He claims that he is a new
Achilles (742), but again the *Iliad* denies the parallel: the scene is
adapted from the Trojan attack on gates in the Greek camp and the
killing of a pair of gigantic Greek defenders.

Vergil says expressly: "If in the very moment of victory now
Turnus had had the concern [for the situation] to break the door-
bolts and let in his friends, then that would have been the last day
of the war and the Trojans" (757–59). Pandarus had shut the door
on Turnus who could have re-opened it after killing the guard.
Instead, madness drove him along, fired with a mad desire for
slaughter. He is obviously no better than the young Euryalus, and
therefore the Italian cause is equally doomed. A mighty beast is not
the most desirable symbol for the Italians. When he first burst into
the camp Turnus resembled a huge tiger among helpless cattle
(730). Now he remains the beast, but the Trojans recover their self-
control: they are like a throng of hunters surrounding a savage lion
(792 ff.). Inch by inch he withdraws, taking his toll of the enemy,
but Juno can do nothing to help him to victory now. So he climbs
to the walls and leaps into the river, which bears him back, clean,
refreshed, and "happy" (818) to his companions. It is an ironic
happiness, for despite his bestial strength and limited success, Tur-
nus has manifested the defects which will eventually cost him his
life and his loyal Italians total defeat.

II BOOK TEN

Vergil does not clarify the temporal sequence between the end
of Book Nine and the beginning of Book Ten, but he implies that a
long day of fighting is concluded as Turnus rejoins his companions
and that a new day begins with the return of Aeneas. It is not ab-
solutely necessary that these two days be successive, but the audience
is certainly entitled to assume such a sequence. Before a satisfactory
scheme can be worked out, of course, it is vital to determine when,
during Aeneas' absence, Turnus' first attack occurred: during the
day Aeneas was at Rome, the day he rode north to Caere, or the day
he apparently spent negotiating with the Etruscans. All this chro-
nology is, however, a minor point, perhaps not fully or intentionally
elaborated by Vergil.[2] There is a similar imprecision in connection
with Aeneas' ship. How did the ship reach the Etruscan coast in
order to bring Aeneas back by sea (see 156)? I assume, at any rate,
that the council of the gods, with which Vergil opens Book Ten,

helps to provide the illusion of time passing and so mark a reasonable break between the fighting in Book Nine and the new conflict inspired in Book Ten by the return of Aeneas.

Jupiter calls the council and protests the war, blaming unnamed gods and asserting that the war conflicts with his express commands (8–9). So far as the *Aeneid* has shown, Jupiter never forbade fighting between Italians and Trojans. On the contrary, when he first unveiled the future for Venus and us, he definitely predicted, without adverse comment, that Aeneas would wage a tremendous war in Italy (1.263). Ever since that point there have been repeated predictions of the war to come. To be sure, nobody wanted the war except Juno and her irrational victims Amata, Turnus, and the volatile mob. Granted, too, the war is an impious, unjust war. Still, this intervention of Jupiter lacks the requisite motivation. Once he has opened discussion, a debate occurs in which Venus tearfully upholds the Trojan cause, while Juno fiercely supports the Italians. There is not much one can say for Venus' arguments: her employment of the "*Iliad* equation" should automatically convict her in our eyes either of passionate irrationality (as bad as Juno's even if in defense of a good cause) or of unscrupulous rhetoric. Her innuendoes against a "certain someone" who has produced so much trouble and her pathetic plea to allow the Trojans to return home do not really get to the heart of the matter. Juno's furious mood guarantees that her contribution will be slight. She twists facts and makes a wild effort—persuasive only to herself and her sympathizers—to link the present conflict with Paris' original sin. The result of the debate, then, is pandemonium in Olympus, comparable to a wild storm at sea (97 ff.). Jupiter, having allowed the deities to get excited, now calms them with a firm declaration: No deity shall intervene in the ensuing day; mortals, by their own ability and luck, will decide the issue, and the Fates will find a way of declaring themselves (113). The stage is now set for the return of Aeneas and its decisive effect on the war.

As morning arrives (256), Aeneas warns his companions to be prepared, then assumes a dramatic position on the lofty stern of his craft, from where he will be clearly visible to friend and foe on shore. The moment is one to which I alluded earlier when commenting on the representation of Actium's battle on Aeneas' shield: like Augustus, he stands high on the poop; like Augustus, he has his head surrounded by light. Implicitly, then, Aeneas is about to face a battle which partakes of some of the symbolic qualities of Actium: he is the representative of Order, the hope of Peace, entering a scene of Disorder and War. From their walls the Trojans greet his arrival with a shout and hurl themselves eagerly into combat; Vergil compares them to a large, noisy flock of cranes on the River Strymon who see a storm coming and rise into the air to escape the winds (264 ff.). The simile seems to anticipate their eventual escape from the tight Italian siege. As for the Italians, they watch Aeneas with wonder and terror; in their eyes he seems to emit flames around his head and to resemble the blood-red, grim light of some comet or the parching, scorching glare of the Dog Star, the source of so many ills to poor mortals.[3] It is no accident that Vergil found a like simile in the *Iliad* at the point where Homer described the return of Achilles to battle after his long absence.

Turnus behaves with the same special bold confidence that he displayed at the metamorphosis of the ships—mistakenly this time, too.[4] In his mouth Vergil places one of those typical battle speeches, complete with appeal to wife and home, which any Roman general might have uttered. And the conclusion, "Fortune helps those who are bold" (284), is a commonplace of Roman morality. Turnus undeniably has many fine qualities about him with which any Roman would feel at home; the tragedy is that his boldness lacks foundation.

Aeneas is the first to attack the Italians and produce an omen of victory by killing Theron (310 ff.). As he continues forward, six more victims of his prowess fall, variously wounded. Vergil describes each killing realistically, but dispassionately, so that we appreciate Aeneas' valor and success without feeling great sympathy for the fallen.[5] It will be different when next we see Aeneas: he will be raging and his victims will be pathetic. For now, though, Vergil leaves Aeneas to summarize the scene of battle at the beachhead and compare it to a storm at sea—to that, for example, seen in Book One—in which the brawling winds battle each other with equal force (357 ff.).

In another sector, Pallas rallies his hard-pressed, faltering Arcadians and performs feats extraordinary for one so young and inexperienced. The wounds he deals are quite ugly, and Vergil increasingly apostrophizes the victims, as though to express his own sympathy and trap our feelings. Pallas first drives his spear into the backbone of Lagus, then yanks it out again as the bones give way (381 ff.). Twins—the delight of their parents because they were so similar—Pallas ironically distinguishes in death, hacking off the head of one, the right arm of the other (390 ff.). The result of all this violence is that the enemy gives way. Vergil, with one of his typically ambiguous similes, compares Pallas to a shepherd who consciously burns off a field and sits calmly surveying the flames do his job; the peaceful rural activities seem far removed from the realities here (405 ff.). Now Pallas performs one more heroic exploit in killing Halaesus. Briefly introducing young Lausus—the son of Mezentius—who plays a similar part for the Italians and will invite important comparison later on (426 ff.), Vergil at last brings Turnus up to dispose quickly of Pallas.

The actual combat is highly one-sided. Pallas throws his spear and grazes the flesh of Turnus; then Turnus hurls his spear mightily, to pierce Pallas' shield and breastplate and plunge into his chest. At this point the actions of Turnus clearly provoke adverse comments and notes of doom from Vergil. The difficulty has been to determine exactly what Turnus has done wrong. When he bestrides the corpse and addresses the Arcadians he is entirely within the heroic convention. What he says cannot be criticized: he comments on the grim solace for Evander in burying his beloved son (sent to death by the father). In no way does he boast or malign Evander. He commits no indignities on the fair body of Pallas. There remains but one thing to blame: he wrenches away the sword belt worn by Pallas, not to dedicate to any god, but to wear proudly as spoils (500). Vergil has already indicated, in what happened to Euryalus, the likely fate of one who spoils a fallen foe. Here he stresses the wrong and the doom of Turnus by various devices, then apostrophizes the dead Pallas; these lines are perhaps the most "subjective" in the whole *Aeneid* (501 ff.). On the sword belt has been worked a famous myth, the murder of young men on their very wedding night by their wives the Danaides. It is a *nefas* of premature death. Turnus, by taking this particular item as spoil and wearing it, is implicitly assuming guilt for a similar crime of premature murder and flaunting his misdeed in the face of Pallas' friends. So Vergil exclaims over the short-sighted overconfidence of people like Turnus. The time will come (namely, in the final confrontation of Turnus and Aeneas) when Turnus will deeply regret taking this accursed spoil from Pallas. For the death of Pallas generates grief not only in his Arcadians and his father Evander, but also in Aeneas. Aeneas' grief is a hero's—angry, fiery, demanding vengeance.

When he learns of Pallas' death, Aeneas is transformed from a methodical, dispassionate conqueror into a savage. His first impulse is to find and kill Turnus (514–15). Failing that, he captures eight Italians, to be slaughtered over the pyre of Pallas. Then he proceeds to rage over the field, mercilessly, tauntingly killing any and all. Mago (521 ff.) pleads by all the basic bonds of *pietas,* and by Aeneas' veneration for dead Anchises and his hopes for Ascanius, to be ransomed and allowed to return alive to his father and son. Aeneas asserts that Turnus has destroyed the very possibility of such arrangements, that Anchises and Ascanius approve his action, then drives his sword up to the hilt into the throat of pleading Mago. A priest comes along (537 ff.): Aeneas stands over him and "immolates" him. The verb belongs significantly to priestly vocabulary and dramatizes the unholy behavior of the hero. Tarquitius approaches boldly (550 ff.), but Aeneas pins his shield against his armor with a spear-throw, then, while the helpless man begs for mercy, hews off his head, and with a kick, sends the headless corpse rolling in the dirt. Not content with that, Aeneas exults that Tarquitius will not go back to his mother for burial, but will be left out as a prey of birds and beasts. For all this barbarity and irresistible violence, Vergil compares Aeneas to a monstrous giant who challenges the very might of Jupiter (565 ff.)! The implication is that our hero has exceeded the limits. More killings follow. In the final pair, Aeneas, ironically called *pius* (591), destroys without pity two brothers, Lucagus and Liger (575 ff.). Another simile epitomizes the destructive, inhuman violence of the man in terms of a ruinous flood (603–4). But the final comment suggests positive results arising from this slaughter. As Aeneas rages floodlike over the fields, the Italians retire in panic and the beleaguered Trojans break out (604–5). For all practical purposes, Aeneas has won the day.

Into less than one hundred lines Vergil has packed a "wrath of Aeneas" which resembles the savage actions, strung over many hundreds of lines, of Achilles after the death of Patroclus. As I pointed out earlier, however, the situation is strikingly different, for Aeneas feels no personal guilt for Pallas' death. And now, as we shall observe, the "wrath" does come under control, quite unlike the suicidal anger of Achilles. Instead of maintaining our attention on Aeneas, Vergil directs it to Turnus (606 ff.), and while we watch him and the subsequent developments, there is time for Aeneas to cool down. Since the killing of Pallas imposes upon Turnus the inevitable confrontation with Aeneas, much of the remainder of the *Aeneid* will exhibit a series of delays and suspended or abortive arrangements designed to postpone the fatal duel. In this instance, Jupiter uses the flimsy excuse of Venus' intervention (608, based apparently on 382) to allow Juno the chance to remove Turnus from the scene.

Then Jupiter inspires Mezentius to replace the Italian leader (689)—an ironic touch, for Mezentius is by definition the "despiser of gods." Lured by a deity he scorns, Mezentius goes to deserved death. When the hated ex-king appears, the Etruscans rush forward to satisfy their vengeful passions. As a warrior, if not as a king, Mezentius exhibits only grandeur, neither the immaturity of Turnus nor the savagery of Aeneas. To bring out the heroic stature, Vergil uses four similes within the space of seventy lines: Mezentius resembles an immovable cliff resisting the furies of winds and waves (that is, the Etruscans, 693 ff.); he is a fearless boar trapped in a net and still terrifying to his hunters (707 ff.); like a hungry lion pouncing upon goat or deer (723 ff.), he drops one Etruscan; and finally, towering above his diminutive foes, he seems a gigantic Orion (763 ff.). But since he replaces Turnus, Mezentius must, prefiguring Turnus' destiny, meet and fall before Aeneas. Only in that encounter does Vergil suggest the blasphemous side of the man, for Mezentius prays to his right hand and his spear as gods (773 ff.). Thus there is a deliberate contrast with Aeneas, whom Vergil calls *pius* (783). Mezentius' "godlike" right arm fails him, but Aeneas seriously wounds his man.

When Mezentius falls wounded, Lausus cannot restrain a groan (788) for the father he loves so much, and tears spring from his eyes. Not content with this description, Vergil intervenes subjectively to apostrophize Lausus, praising his self-sacrifice. Rushing forward with others to assail Aeneas, the brave Lausus gives his companions the chance to pull Mezentius off the field. This initial success goes to the head of the boy—Vergil calls him *demens*, senseless (813)—and infuriates Aeneas, who, however, recognizes *pietas* and so tries to warn Lausus to retire (811–12). When Lausus persists, Aeneas runs him through, then stops, shocked by what he has done, groaning, pitying poor Lausus. As Vergil interprets it, the exigencies of battle have pitted *pietas* (824) against *pietas* (826); Aeneas' basic humanity has not been able to spare the boy. But it can at least function now. Here we are meant to contrast the heartless, unthinking treatment of Pallas by Turnus, remembering that Vergil bracketed Pallas and Lausus. Aeneas lifts up the corpse tenderly and hands it back, armor and all, for honorable burial. No looting, no boasting.

The death of Mezentius is one of those special masterpieces of Vergil. He succeeds in redeeming the "blasphemer," reducing him to the simple figure of a grieving father who blames himself for his son's death. The humbled words of Mezentius have tragic depth (846 ff.). At the end, when he welcomes Aeneas' death stroke, he has but one request: to be buried with Lausus (906). Vergil does not report Aeneas' answer. We are left to decide whether the warrior, like the poet, would have been generous.

◄§ VII ◊►

TURNUS OR AENEAS? BOOKS
ELEVEN AND TWELVE

The question in the title of this chapter assumes two forms. First, there is the suspense plot: will Turnus or Aeneas win? Second, we must evaluate the event: should Turnus or Aeneas win, or which do we prefer? Both forms of the question are fundamental to Vergil's purposes in his final two books. In Book Eleven, he dramatizes Turnus' efforts to combat defeatism among the Latins, to revive conflict rather than negotiate with the Trojans. When hostilities resume, the strategy of Turnus proves an utter failure because of Camilla's death and his own impatience. Early in Book Twelve it seems that the long-postponed duel is to be formally arranged and the war thus settled. Again, however, the spirit of Disorder prevails in the interests of Juno and her human representative Turnus. While Aeneas, treacherously wounded, is compelled to withdraw for medical attention, Turnus seizes his unholy opportunity to violate the treaty. As his career of slaughtering takes him farther and farther from his responsibility, he leaves Latinus' city exposed. By attacking it, Aeneas compels Turnus to fight or resign all hope of honor. Aeneas of course wins. But when the suspense plot has been concluded, the second crucial question remains: do we prefer Turnus or Aeneas?

I BOOK ELEVEN

Approximately halfway through Book Eleven, as the Italians prepare to engage the Trojans in another day of fighting, Vergil pauses to estimate the behavior of Turnus by means of a simile. We are to think of a spirited horse which has broken its tether, escaped from its stall, and having reached open field and freedom, raced off to join the mares or to splash in a nearby river; it stretches its neck and neighs exuberantly, and its long mane dances over its neck and shoulders. What does the poet convey about the valiant Italian leader with this image (492 ff.)? The spirited activity of the horse obviously corresponds with the animation of Turnus as he eagerly moves out to battle. Like the horse, he loves movement and action; he entertains not the slightest hesitation, and like the horse, he strikes a handsome figure of heroism among his fellow Italians. That is the positive side of the simile: Turnus the hero in the conventional pose of the eager young warrior. There is, however, a negative side to the simile which implies criticism of this "heroism" for its selfish irresponsibility, for its very recklessness and unthinking indulgence in mere physical activity. Remember, Vergil begins the simile by noting that the horse has broken its tether and escaped from its stall. Tether and stall qualify the so-called "freedom" of the horse and all its consequent movements. What about Turnus' "freedom"? He, too, has broken his tether and escaped the place where he should be, namely, the council of the Italians which is attempting to arrive at a rational and less costly conclusion to the war than so far has been achieved by hand-to-hand combat. It is implicit in the treatment of the image that, just as the horse is indulging itself in wild play contrary to the wishes of its master, so Turnus' martial activities represent illicit behavior; and just as the horse will inevitably be caught and tied up again, so Turnus will be brought up short. His way of war is self-indulgence; his responsibility demands of him a more ordered method of combat: a duel with Aeneas to decide the whole issue.

Ultimately Vergil developed the horse simile from one used twice in the *Iliad* to characterize the attitude of Paris, and then of Hector, at irresponsible moments.[1] Although it adds to our appreciation of this moment to recognize the features of irresponsible Paris and reckless Hector—Trojans both—in Turnus, Vergil has given us ample scope for interpretation in the simile and the lines that lead up to it. For he has described fully the way Turnus arms himself before dashing out, like the horse, to the field of battle, and in that description he has inserted the key epithet *furens* (486) to comment on Turnus' wildness. Madness is nothing new in Turnus; in this book, however, it remains unvaried in every episode. Shortly after this scene Turnus will retire to lay an ambush for Aeneas in a mountain pass. When he emerges, having accomplished nothing, he will be *furens* again (901). His fury will be motivated by the defeat that the Italians have sustained without him. At the same time the poet will comment on that fury by noting its bad timing; had Turnus controlled himself a little, he might have caught Aeneas, who now emerges unharmed from the pass where Turnus has laid his trap. Thus Book Eleven ends by emphasizing the inadequacy of

Turnus' furious way of battle. Earlier, in portraying Turnus in the Italian council, Vergil had commented on other aspects of this inadequacy. Let us look briefly at that important council.

A new figure emerges in Book Eleven to function as ambiguous foil to Turnus among the Italians. Drances first appears when the Italians send an embassy to Aeneas after the bloody fighting of the previous day to arrange a brief truce which will permit both sides to bury their dead. When Aeneas responds far more generously than they anticipated and urges an ordered settlement by a duel between himself and Turnus, Drances suddenly speaks up with words of praise for Aeneas and spiteful sneers for Turnus (122 ff.). Here begins a complex political situation, for we can agree with Drances' estimate of Aeneas' magnanimity, but Vergil makes sure that we do not fully approve of the dispraise of Turnus. Drances' own unattractive personality obtrudes too much in his judgment of his political foe. (The Romans found this situation so credible that some even detected here allusions to familiar Roman politicians.)[2] When the Italians assemble a week or so later to discuss their crisis, Drances and Turnus are the foremost speakers, and each is quali- fied—Drances by his jealousy, Turnus by his fundamental violence.

The Italian crisis consists of two elements: (1) the general feeling of grief and defeatism occasioned by Aeneas' recent victory and the many corpses which the Italians had to burn; (2) the particular shock when the Greek Diomedes refused to join their "crusade" against the Trojans. Drances had been active in a vicious propa- ganda campaign against Turnus (220), but Turnus had many sup- porters, including the queen, to balance this opposition. Between these two factions Latinus attempted to tread a sensible path, but he was too old to assert himself effectively. As first speaker at the council, he weakly proposes terms that are not likely to please any- one: namely, to give the Trojans a large parcel of land to the west —where they can settle and enjoy rights equal to those of the Latins—or, if they prefer, to help them sail elsewhere with new ships. Such terms affront Turnus and the war party, yet they can- not satisfy the peace party or Aeneas, to whom less is now offered in his moment of military advantage than when, lacking allies, he arrived pacifically. Recognizing this, Drances devotes his efforts to humiliating and enraging Turnus. But before he speaks, Vergil intrudes with further facts about Drances (336 ff.) which compel us to question the speaker's motives and his proposals. It is a clever speech. Drances first insinuates that Turnus prevents free speech and compels others to fight his war—which is not true. He then moves to his amendment of Latinus' proposal: Lavinia (whom Turnus passionately loves) should be offered to Aeneas, as before, as a token of lasting peace. Next, anticipating Turnus' reaction, he affects to plead with Latinus not to yield to the violence of anyone (354). His peroration is an insidious apostrophe to that "anyone," which we might modernize somewhat like this: "Give us peace; there is no security in war. Since you are beaten, give up. Or if you insist on war, take full responsibility and fight Aeneas. Stop using our boys for your unscrupulous political advantage!"

It is a cruel fact that Drances' words, spoken for the wrong reasons, serve to dramatize Turnus' inadequacy. The very violence which Drances warned us about (and of course deliberately provoked) erupts in Turnus' hot, angry reply (376 ff.). Like every man of action, he utterly despises the man of mere words.[3] Yet it is significant that Drances made his telling points in thirty-three lines, whereas Turnus rages half-incoherently through twice that number, or sixty-seven lines. Ignoring the concrete proposal concerning Lavinia, he devotes half his speech to an attempt to discredit his political foe. When he at last comments on Latinus' proposal, he can only assert unconvincingly that hope does remain for total victory. His peroration is a passionate answer to the sneers of Drances again: he will face Aeneas boldly even though the Trojan surpass Achilles and wear armor also made by Vulcan!

Nothing has been decided, and feelings are running high on both sides while Latinus watches impotently, when Aeneas' sudden offensive provides a dubious resolution of the impasse. As the Trojan-Etruscan army approaches, Turnus seizes his chance, sweeps aside others' hesitations, galvanizes the majority into warlike fervor, furiously dons his armor, and rushes out like the freed horse of the simile. Clearly, his fury has dictated the wrong "heroic" alternative. After his brave peroration, we might have expected him to engage Aeneas in a duel, but he does not. Similarly, in Book Twelve, we shall see him capitalizing on a moment of confusion to disrupt another opportunity for the duel and a negotiated, virtually bloodless peace. Wild Amata has her way too: she leads the Latin women to the temple of Minerva to call down imprecations upon Aeneas, the "Phrygian brigand" (484).[4] It is another paradigm of impious fury in action.

The ambush which Turnus contrives can hardly be described as heroic. It does, however, remove him once more from action and replace him with a substitute who, like Mezentius, by dying in battle, anticipates Turnus' death.[5] Camilla is a woman fighting among men, like an Amazon, but she has no clear motives for fighting, and when her womanhood asserts itself over militant purposes, she is doomed. After killing a series of enemies, she becomes preoccupied with the finery of her latest victim, which glitters with desirable gold. Vergil allows us alternative assessments of her motives at this fatal moment (778 ff.): she may have intended to dedicate the gold in a temple, or she may have hoped to wear it herself. In any case, afire with an all too feminine love of plunder (782), she forgets the battle and presents an easy target to the archer Arruns. We are meant to recall what happened to Euryalus, what mistake Turnus made with Pallas' spoils. And as a further foreshadowing of Turnus' doom, Vergil assigns to Camilla's death the same line (831) which will report Turnus' and so end the epic (12.952): "With a groan life flees raging to the shades below."

If Camilla functions as a substitute for Turnus, Aeneas acts implicitly to emphasize the deficiencies of the Italian, not least in this very matter of using spoils. As the book opens, Aeneas stands before what the Romans called a trophy: a tree trunk clothed with the armor of dead Mezentius. All these spoils are being dedicated to Mars. Vergil allows us no alternative here: Aeneas has not been tempted—like Euryalus, Turnus, or Camilla—to don the glittering spoils of his foe; he has immediately given all to the god of war. Standing before this trophy and addressing his Trojans and allies, Aeneas is the figure of the great Roman leader.

In his attitude toward the war, too, Aeneas stands in sharp contrast with Turnus. The victory of the previous day gives him confidence that the war can be quickly won, as he proclaims to his men. However, he recognizes what war costs and expresses bitter regret, in particular for dead Pallas. Such humane awareness makes him not only willing to concede the truce to the Italians but also eager to limit the destructiveness of the warfare by means of a decisive duel between himself and Turnus. The duel is the ordered way of fighting and appropriate to Aeneas; random fighting and killing is the disorderly method of Turnus. Dead Pallas is in a way an epitome of the futile victims of Turnus, cut down like a violet or hyacinth in the flower of his youth (67–68). For a Turnus who thinks that such victories and victims justify the implicit exultation of selfish spoiling, it is inevitable that the long-delayed duel, when it eventually arrives, will be, at least in part, a moment of justice.

II BOOK TWELVE

The events of Book Twelve take place the night and day following the second military defeat of the Italians. There are three large sections: 1–310 (the abortive treaty, its elaborate preparations, and its disruption through the agency of Juno); 311–696 (the futile battle which arises while Turnus avoids the duel with Aeneas); 697–952 (the duel ending in Turnus' death). Throughout the book Vergil offers us implicit and explicit comparisons between Turnus and Aeneas: for example, as the two prepare separately for the truce arranged duel (81 ff.), respond to the violation of the truce (311 ff.), and finally meet to fight the duel (681 ff.). Furthermore, Vergil uses many important similes and symbolic episodes to interpret the action and suggest its complexities. Finally, there are more Homeric allusions in this book than in any other except Book One. Anyone who discusses Book Twelve—surely the most magnificent book of the entire epic—must do so with diffidence.[6]

Vergil opens the book with an important description of Turnus. Realizing the defeat and the responsibility he must now face in the eyes of all, Turnus shows an implacable, fiery violence. He resembles a lion in the territory of Carthage, wounded by hunters: the lion shakes its mane, fearlessly breaks off the spear that has wounded him, and with a roar from its bloody mouth prepares to fight to the death. Such is the violence that grows in the fired heart of Turnus. Lions are magnificent beasts; they are beasts, however. The Romans admired their strength, but did not indulge in Walt Disney fancies about their ravenous hunger and ruinous, murderous violence. Furthermore, Vergil reminds us here, especially by his reference to Carthage, of the metaphorical cluster with which he opened Book Four and prepared for the death of Dido: she too was possessed by a destructive force. The same Latin phrase occurs here to describe the lion, roaring from its bloody mouth, as earlier has been assigned to the very incarnation of Disorder, *Furor impius,* raging to be released (1.296). Even if we do not recall the phrase, the connection between Turnus and *Furor impius* is not hard to grasp.

The duel which Turnus now hotheadedly demands is no more necessary than renewal of the combat was necessary in Book Eleven. The obvious alternative is a treaty of peace to end bloodshed and resign to Aeneas what has been offered him on his first arrival. But Turnus must choose the way of war: he has nothing left but his warrior's code and the honor that goes with it. Vergil deliberately reminds us of the scene in the *Iliad* when Hector was facing a similar choice and decided to encounter Achilles before the walls of Troy. There are some crucial distinctions, though, which attenuate the resemblance of Turnus to noble Hector, for Hector had not started the war, would derive no personal advantage from it, and plainly acted from a combination of patriotism, honor, and shame. Turnus' case is considerably weaker, his mood far less rationally heroic or patriotic. Furthermore, the man Turnus intends to encounter approaches him with few of the angry, murderous, almost suicidal passions that motivated Achilles. When Latinus urges Turnus to give up the fight entirely, Turnus replies with violence (45). When Amata pleads with him to save his life, Turnus is distracted by the sight of Lavinia blushing and weeping.[7] Confused by his love (70), he heatedly demands the duel even more insistently. It is set for the next morning.

Vergil keeps our attention on the behavior of Turnus (81 ff.). In twenty-six lines he builds up a dramatic portrait of irrationality, then juxtaposes a laconic six lines to compare Aeneas. Turnus rushes back to his quarters, checks over horses and all his gear, tries on his special sword, brandishes his spear and wildly apostrophizes it, under the impetus of fury which makes him seem to emit sparks from mouth and eyes (101 ff.). The torch of Allecto, his peculiar symbol, is obviously at work. Now he is compared to another beast, a bull readying itself for combat. By contrast, Aeneas, though indeed savagely eager for the duel, spends his time analyzing the political problems of the truce and consoling Ascanius (107 ff.). His is controlled passion, and Vergil does not assign him any animal simile.

At dawn the next day, careful preparations are being made to set up altars for the treaty ceremonies and to mark off the field of combat. Here is a scene of order, a rational attempt by men to limit the vain carnage of war, and Juno cannot endure the sight. Unable to intervene directly because of Jupiter's express commands, she evades responsibility by spurring Turnus' sister Juturna to disrupt the truce (158). Left in a state of emotional confusion, "wounded" (160), Juturna inevitably does the work of disorder appropriate to her wild brother and disorderly Juno. The ceremonies start. First *pius Aeneas* (175) solemnly swears to abide by the terms of the treaty, either to win and settle down without dominating the Italians tyranically or to die fighting and so cause his Trojans to retire forever from Latium. Then Latinus swears that the treaty will always be sacred among the Italians (195 ff.). Turnus, too, must make his oath, and Vergil describes him moving forward to the altar (219–20), but we never hear Turnus' words. We may choose to believe that he did swear, and so is foresworn later when he fights, or that the violation of the treaty occurs before he has made the oath. At any rate, Juturna now seizes her opportunity.

The sight of young Turnus approaching the altar by which stands the seasoned warrior Aeneas, exuding confidence and righteousness, disturbs his people the Rutulians. When Juturna, posing as a warrior, pushes through the ranks with inflammatory words, murmurs of dissatisfaction start. She ignites them to action by contriving an omen in the sky: an eagle starts to snatch away a gorgeous swan, but abandons the attempt when other birds swarm after him (245 ff.). An augur Tolumnius, qualified by his office to explain such portents, interprets it as follows: Turnus is the swan, Aeneas the eagle, and they, the Italians, will be the other birds forcing villainous Aeneas to release his prey (see 261 ff.). The interpretation satisfies the Italians, who are predisposed to favor any omen for battle, but Vergil has said that they are deceived (246). Does he mean that the counterfeit omen tricks them by not corresponding to the events, even though legitimately interpreted; or does he imply that the omen, because ambiguous, leads to misinterpretation from Tolumnius? Remember that Turnus has already been compared to an eagle snatching a swan (see 9.563–64); that Aeneas' fleet after Juno's storm evoked a bird omen about a flock of swans disrupted by an eagle (see 1.393 ff.). It is at least possible that Turnus is the eagle here, Lavinia the swan, and the Trojans the bird swarm which compels him—as in fact Turnus is compelled—to abandon Lavinia.

When violence shatters the order of the treaty ceremonies, the question arises: what will Aeneas and Turnus do? They are the supreme commanders; they agreed to a duel; Aeneas at least has sworn an oath, and Turnus certainly either did or was about to do so. Thus they might have insisted on the terms of the treaty, stopped the mutual bloodshed, and staged their duel as planned. It is plain that Aeneas wants to do precisely this; Vergil displays him as *pius Aeneas* again (311) acting in sharp contrast to the mob. Unarmed, unhelmeted, Aeneas advances into the field and tries to check his own troops. A mysterious arrow flies through the air and wounds him painfully in the leg. Who did it? Nobody claims the credit (322). However, from what Juno says later in 815, we might legitimately suspect the hand of Juturna. The wound forces Aeneas to limp off the field, supported by his friends, and prevents him from exerting discipline upon the Trojans, Arcadians, and Etruscans under his command. It also fires Turnus with hope (325), making him ignore his responsibility to fight the duel. Here, then, is another important contrast between Aeneas and Turnus to affect our ultimate evaluation. As Turnus sends his chariot flying into battle, Vergil compares him to bloody Mars himself (331 ff.). Can this incarnation of war be halted, constrained the way *Furor impius* must be (according to Augustan symbolism)?

While Turnus carries out his slaughter far and wide, raging destructively like the Thracian winds (365 ff.), Aeneas is being tended by doctors. They, however, have no success against the barbed arrow lodged in his leg until Venus intervenes. Free at last to return to the field, Aeneas dons his armor eagerly, embraces his son, and addresses to him words which reveal his state of mind. There is no violence or passion in what he says, but resignation and a determination to face his toils and display his manliness (435 ff.). Fortune has never been his to enjoy personally, nor would he ask for fortune before courage (*virtus*). His return produces a shiver of terror among the Italians (447–48). Like farmers watching a storm come in from the sea that will create havoc among their trees and crops, they watch his approach (451 ff.). In fact, though Tolumnius falls and pays the price for initiating hostilities (460), Aeneas himself kills no one at first: his sole concern remains to find Turnus and compel him to fight that duel (464 ff.) He still intends to abide by the treaty.

To prevent the encounter, inasmuch as her other efforts have failed to defeat Aeneas, Juturna replaces Turnus' charioteer and drives him rapidly to another part of the field, wherever Aeneas is not. The simile which Vergil contrives to represent her concern (473 ff.) conveys with full sympathy her anxiety: he compares her devious course through the enemy to the flitting of a mother swallow as it passes among the columns of a wealthy man's atrium bringing food to its nestlings. The irony is, of course, that Turnus is no nestling, and the field of battle is no serenely splendid Roman house. Aeneas continues his monotonous search—Vergil suggests a "hunt"—until Messapus and others, attacking him spontaneously, compel him to become aggressive. He calls upon the gods to witness his honorable behavior and the actions of others who break the treaty (496), then advances, a fearful figure, now prepared to battle without distinction against any and all enemies. Here is another juncture when Vergil encourages us to compare the two mighty warriors in separate parts of the field (500 ff.). The Trojan hero (*Troius heros,* 502) kills each of his opponents, saying nothing, exhibiting no feelings, and content to leave the corpse alone. Turnus, in one case, hews off the heads of brothers and barbarously hangs them to gush blood on his chariot (511). Bloodthirsty Mars again. As Vergil surveys the scene of the field where the duel should have settled the war, it seems one ruinous, restless battle (552).

Since it is obvious that he can never catch up with Turnus, Aeneas needs some way of bringing Turnus to him. That is provided by a suggestion of Venus: attack the city of Latinus, compel Turnus to come to its defense. The idea has been perhaps adumbrated in Aeneas' strategy of Book Eleven, but now the attack really comes. There is a general assault on gates and walls with normal weapons and fire. Aeneas has shouted to his men that they must demand the fulfillment of the treaty by use of flames (573), and we can understand that he has been pushed to this violent strategy. However, Vergil reminds us through his simile (587 ff.) of other factors. Aeneas resembles, he claims, a shepherd who is smoking out of their hive a swarm of bees. The confusion created by the shepherd parallels the pandemonium in Latinus' city. We may or may not recall what Aeneas' presence in Carthage did to the thriving bee community described in simile at his arrival (1.430 ff.); in any case, we cannot be so dispassionate about what Aeneas does to people in Italy and Carthage as the shepherd would justly be about mere bees (for all their "human" organization).

Smoke towers into the sky from burning houses. Watching this disaster, Queen Amata irrationally leaps to the conclusion that Turnus is dead; otherwise he would be defending them. The tragic creature (*infelix*, 598) hangs herself, and here, as she wildly laments her mother's death, we encounter Lavinia for the last time in the *Aeneid* (605). We never know how she feels about Aeneas, only how much she suffers because of her mother's domineering ways. Far off, on the distant field, Turnus begins to feel some unease, hearing dim cries from the city (614 ff.). When a wounded messenger arrives to report the grave peril of the city, the inclination of Latinus to surrender, and the suicide of Amata, Turnus goes wild with a confusion of shame, grief, love, manly resolution, and insane frustration (665 ff.). As he turns, undecided (*turbidus*, 671), to look at the city, flames well through the storeys and rise above the summit of a tower that he himself had constructed. The symbolism is obvious: all his plans are going up in smoke; the fire which Allecto planted in him is destroying him. Back he must go to confront Aeneas. "Let me rage out this rage of mine," he says to his sister (680), jumps to the ground, and dashes wildly across the field.

Dramas and dramatic poetry can make suicidal behavior grandiose, as Vergil does here, but the continuous state of irrationality in which Turnus has existed up to this point does not really make that "rage" of his admirable or desirable. Again Vergil invites us to compare our two men, using similes to assess their behavior before the duel. Turnus careers madly across the plain like a boulder, loosened from its mountain, which plunges erratically down the slope and out onto the plain, cutting a wide swathe of destruction (684 ff.). Aeneas breaks off his attack and proceeds confidently toward Turnus, while his armor thunders menacingly, looking as gigantic and majestic as Mounts Athos, Eryx, or the highest summit of the Appennines, which tower into the sky unperturbed by the thunder in the oak trees on their flanks.

While battle ceases and other warriors give way to open up an area for the duel, the two move forward, then immediately launch their spears (711). Both having missed, they close with their swords. Vergil interrupts with a simile (715 ff.): the two heroes resemble bulls battling for control of a herd.[8] The poet's refusal to discriminate parallels his technique in the next scene: he describes Jupiter weighing the fates of Turnus and Aeneas without revealing the result (725 ff.). But the action implies the truth, for Turnus' sword shatters on the armor of Aeneas. In his wild state of mind that morning, he seized the wrong sword, leaving behind him the special one made for Daunus by Vulcan (see 90).[9] Like Cacus in 8.223, he flees faster than the wind (733), his folly discovered. Aeneas tries to hunt him down in order to stab him with his own sword, but his wound slows him down. For a moment the scene resembles the pursuit of a deer by a hound (749 ff.); but I do not think that Vergil intends us to release our sympathies in a flood for the poor deer, because he does not prejudice the case with any subjective *infelix* or *miser*. Turnus begs his friends to get him his sword; Aeneas threatens anyone who tries. So the hunt turns into a "race" (763 ff.), whose grim prize is the life of Turnus.[10]

Realizing that he can never catch Turnus, Aeneas decides to recover his spear and hit the enemy from a distance. Vergil carefully describes the oleaster in which the spear is lodged. Once it was sacred to Faunus (a Latin deity) and adorned with countless votive offerings; now, in order to make the field open for undisturbed battle, the Trojans have indiscriminately defiled the sacred tree, hacking off its branches, reducing it to a naked trunk (766 ff.). It suggests the ruthless results of the Trojan presence—but remember that the war was forced on them—and we are not surprised when Faunus prevents Aeneas from pulling out the spear. However, when Juturna restores to Turnus his sword, Venus frees Aeneas' spear. We are back almost where we began.

Vergil leaves the two champions facing each other, catching their breath, and transports us to Olympus to overhear the reconciliation of Jupiter and Juno. Although Jupiter bars further interference from Juno, he makes concessions too, so that she can be contented with a victory of Aeneas that will, in effect, produce the final "death" of Troy (that is, the birth of Rome). She retires, happy for the first time (841). How wonderful it would be if human beings could achieve so complete and happy a reconciliation. It cannot be, it seems. Jupiter implies the tragic situation when he dispatches to Juturna his horrible messenger, which evokes images of Tartarus, Night, the Furies (846), terrified poor mortals (850; see 10.274), poisoned Parthian arrows—the Parthians were dreaded foreign enemies of Augustus (856 ff.)—and screech owls hooting around graves at night (862 ff.). Bewailing her brother and the cruel gift which compels her to live on after Turnus, Juturna leaves the scene.

Our attention returns to the two champions. Aeneas brandishes his spear and asks Turnus why he hesitates—an ironic echo of Turnus' sneer in Eleven? Though Turnus has his sword, he can hardly use it. Instead he tries to pick up a gigantic boulder and crush Aeneas beneath it—with nightmarish lack of success (896 ff.). As Turnus falters, Aeneas throws his spear, pierces the other's shield, armor, and leg. Turnus falls, and a roar goes up from the crowd— to remind us of the interested "herd" of the earlier simile.[11] Now Aeneas can use his sword. In Turnus' last words, as he unflinchingly faces that sword, we recognize a great man, clearheaded and morally aware. He admits his deserts, signals before all his utter defeat, concedes Lavinia. Asking Aeneas to remember Anchises and consider the feelings of a father, he requests that he be returned to Daunus alive, or if that must be, dead (but at least honorably). "Do not strain to continue these feelings of hatred," he concludes.

Here is the most poignant moment of the epic, abounding in traps for the sentiments and one-sided interpretations. Aeneas hesitates, then drives his sword into Turnus' chest. The last lines speak of victorious Aeneas standing hotly (951) over the corpse of this man who has created so much disorder; of the chill that creeps over Turnus' limbs, the life that groans and rages as it flees to the shades below. Why does Vergil emphasize Aeneas' anger? Does he really wish to leave the impression that Aeneas has turned into the fury-ridden monster (compare 946) that in theory was destroyed in Turnus? Is he redeeming Turnus and forcing us to depreciate Aeneas' victory? The words which the poet selects for this moment are significant, and his silence can also be construed as eloquent.

To begin with, Aeneas' hesitation is striking testimony to his humanity and *pietas*. Nowhere else in the epic has any warrior listened to a fallen foe's pleas for mercy. Every strand of the plot has been leading toward the death of Turnus. In pausing before the fatal stroke, Aeneas reveals that he is not merely a warrior seeking the easy, obvious conclusion to a duel. When, however, he sees the sword belt of Pallas, the charity he feels toward Turnus comes into violent conflict with the greater *pietas* controlling the relation with Evander and dead Pallas. We may not agree with Aeneas' action on behalf of the dead—for killing Turnus accomplishes nothing, in our terms, for Pallas. That, however, is not the way Vergil thinks. He condemned Turnus' folly at the time of Pallas' death and clearly predicted this moment of reckoning. Turnus, in wearing the sword belt, flaunted his cheap victory in the face of Aeneas, the substitute father of Pallas (commissioned by Evander to avenge the death). The bond of *pietas* to Pallas could not be denied; the very memory of Anchises to which Turnus appealed would support this avenging of Pallas.

We can also say that the momentum of Book Twelve leads to this death. Not until the second phase of the duel (887 ff.) do we really see Turnus as anything but the human representative of *furor impius,* and by then it is too late to do anything except partly redeem him, much as Dido was redeemed in Book Four, Mezentius in Book Ten. We can hardly believe that Turnus will go back to Ardea, if spared, and serenely find himself another wife with whom he can live happily ever after. Nor does it seem credible that the war can conclude without his death. Vergil recognized, though with regret, what we also perceive: that men can rarely achieve a reconciliation such as that of Jupiter and Juno.[12]

There is, then, both justice and truth in the killing of Turnus. The question as to whether we prefer Aeneas or Turnus should be answerable: Aeneas is preferable. But Vergil has lavished details on Aeneas' emotions in killing Turnus which complicate our attitude toward Aeneas. Aeneas is really the central problem of the conclusion, Aeneas described as the angry killer rather than the much-celebrated victor. Although it is true that Vergil ended Books Four and Ten with the deaths of disordered Dido and Mezentius rather than lines about heroic Aeneas, that fact only tells us that Vergil regularly avoided final heroics. Why here? The only passage where Aeneas may possibly reach such paroxysms of wrath is at the time of Pallas' death. However, even there Vergil does not pack his details so densely. Thus the anger of Aeneas, "fired by furies and terrible in wrath," is emphatic. He may claim that Pallas "immolates" Turnus, but the metaphor cannot conceal the person of the real killer.

Vergil, I think, has caught a truth in this representation of angry, murderous Aeneas. Killing Turnus is a victory for the cause, but not for Aeneas. In this final struggle between aspects of *pietas*, Aeneas can only be the loser. Triumphant he should never be; angry, I feel that I understand him better. It is his final assertion against (enslavement to?) the destiny that has almost dehumanized him, the final proof by Vergil that *pius Aeneas* is not passive, but more tragic than Dido and Turnus together.[13]

⊷§ VIII §⊷

TRANSLATION AND
VERGILIAN STYLE

It is the common experience of teachers dealing with humanities courses or courses in Greek and Roman literature that the *Aeneid* fails to impress the average student, to a large degree because of the inadequacy of all translations. Not that the translators lack ability. Indeed, some of them are distinguished poets. But Vergil placed insuperable problems in the way of translators: his style, an essential aspect of the total epic, has not been, and probably cannot be translated.[1] Unlike Homer, Vergil did not produce a poem which would be a "good story" in itself. Anyone can enjoy the *Odyssey*, for example, whether presented in Victorian prose or in racy modern verse; its power does not depend so heavily on the techniques of oral composition. When Vergil wrote the *Aeneid*, the different times and his own special talents demanded a thoroughly conscious exploitation of every relevant stylistic technique. The art of the *Aeneid*, therefore, involves many technical skills which Vergil, starting from the experiments of his predecessors, developed to near-perfection. Although it is possible and important to analyze the broad themes and imagery of the epic (where the translation preserves them), we inevitably miss in translations the full power of his poem, for we but dimly glimpse Vergil's mastery of word choice, word arrangement, sound and rhythm. Consequently we miss the very implications of such conscious style. When Vergil's father made financial sacrifices to send him away to school, he intended his son to be a lawyer. Vergil obediently studied rhetoric for many years, as most young upper-class Romans did, but he disappointed his father. Instead of employing that rhetoric for *practical* and profitable results in a legal career, he put it to even better use in forging the style of the *Aeneid*, the despair of the admiring translator. In this chapter, I shall discuss some salient qualities of Vergilian style.

To make points as concretely as possible, it seems wise to select a short passage from the Latin and analyze the problems it poses for translators. We have just discussed the conclusion of the *Aeneid,* making only minimal reference to the Latin. Now let us look at the last fourteen lines as Latin that must be rendered as fully and sympathetically as possible. Here is the Latin:

> stetit acer in armis
> Aeneas, volvens oculos, dextramque repressit;
> 940 et iam iamque magis cunctantem flectere sermo
> coeperat, infelix umero cum adparuit alto
> balteus et notis fulserunt cingula bullis
> Pallantis pueri, victum quem vulnere Turnus
> straverat atque umeris inimicum insigne gerebat.
> 945 ille, oculis postquam saevi monimenta doloris
> exuviasque hausit, furiis accensus et ira
> terribilis: "tune hinc spoliis indute meorum
> eripiare mihi? Pallas te hoc vulnere, Pallas
> immolat, et poenam scelerato ex sanguine sumit."
> 950 hoc dicens ferrum adverso sub pectore condit
> fervidus. ast illi solvuntur frigore membra,
> vitaque cum gemitu fugit indignata sub umbras.

I intend to make points about Vergilian word order and the structure of the hexameter line, and therefore I must give the reader a translation which I have deliberately made to reflect as closely as possible the original word order. I have also marked the line endings.

> He stood fierce in armor/Aeneas, his eyes moving, and his right hand he checked;/ and now more and more, as he hesitated, to move him the speech/had begun, when—a thing of cruel misfortune—on [Turnus'] shoulder there appeared at the top/the baldric, the sword belt glittering with its familiar bosses,/belonging to Pallas, the boy whom Turnus had defeated and with [mortal] wound/felled; on his shoulders [Turnus] his enemy's ornament was wearing./Aeneas, when with his eyes this reminder of savage grief,/these spoils he had drunk in, with fury fired and by anger/frightful [cried out]: "Are you then, wearing the spoils of my friend,/to be snatched away from me? Pallas with this wound, Pallas/sacrifices you, exacting punishment from your criminal blood."/ So saying, his sword in the chest turned toward him he buries /hotly. As for Turnus, relaxed with chill are his limbs,/and his life with a groan flees, raging at injustice, below to the shades.

The first point is obvious but important. As an inflected language, Latin revealed the relationships between words by noun, adjective, and verb endings rather than by word position. Thus, particularly in poetry, Latin permitted considerable freedom of word order. Exploiting this "freedom," Vergil could make it a means for special emphasis. In ordinary Latin prose, there are certain expectable sequences: noun-subjects tend to precede their verbs; adjectives usually follow their nouns closely; conjunctions and relative pronouns begin clauses and verbs end them. Now consider the effect sought by Vergil from the unusual position of five adjectives in this passage: *acer, infelix, inimicum, saevi,* and *fervidus.*[2] How is the translator to catch the emphasis when English has only one position for adjectives?

Vergil's adjectives constitute a particularly effective element of his rhetoric because (unlike Homer's) they are regularly selected to color the individual passage.[3] We may think of the hero as a standardized *pius Aeneas,* but in fact Aeneas receives that special epithet only twenty times. Moreover, as I have indicated in discussing such passages as 4.393, 10.826, and 12.311, even that familiar adjective conveys a sense appropriate to its own context. Vergil does not call Aeneas *pius* in these final lines. Even though the act of avenging Pallas could be construed as a form of *pietas,* the poet uses quite different epithets: *acer, furiis accensus, ira terribilis, fervidus.* These words conjure up a particular impression about Aeneas, all the more forcefully since they rarely apply to him elsewhere (and never in such density). Clearly, we are not to think that we are watching the usual Aeneas; this is a man transformed by anger enough to kill a defenseless enemy despite his appeal for humane treatment.

To increase the effectiveness of adjectives and other words, Vergil weaves them together into a pattern of themes. In this part of Book Twelve, the significant thing is that Aeneas receives epithets which generally appear in thematic clusters around his enemies. It is Aeneas' function to be *pius,* to bring peace and order where disorder has prevailed. Fire and fury, as we have seen, characterize disorder, not the ideal qualities of Aeneas. Juno, Dido, and Turnus are fired and furious, and for that reason they cannot prevail. Now, using fire and fury to characterize Aeneas, Vergil sheds an ironic light on Aeneas' "victory." As he kills Turnus and establishes a peace that enables Rome to come into existence, Aeneas has, at least momentarily, succumbed to the very malign forces he has been trying passionately to combat.

Now let us return to the five adjectives and the practical problems facing translators. There is no insuperable difficulty in *acer* (938): Humphries gets it exactly ("fierce in his arms"); Lewis strays off somewhat freely to "on the edge of the stroke"; Copley puts *acer* and *dextram* together to produce "Aeneas checked a savage blow." [4] Now since *acer* is ambivalent in Latin usage, it should not be prejudiced by the English word "savage," an unequivocally negative term. Aeneas behaves eagerly, keenly, fiercely, exactly as this moment in the duel requires. Soon enough, his keenness turns to murderous anger which could merit the epithet "savage." In 938, such a word is premature.

The second chief adjective is *infelix* (941). It shows up clearly the inadequacy of all translation, for nobody can capture in English the full effect of the word's position (radically separated from *balteus*) and its twofold application. The strategy of all three of the translators listed above is to abandon the effort to catch the initial pathetic notes and instead to place the word in final position, as a doublet with the phrase *inimicum insigne* of 944. Both Humphries and Lewis in addition perceive and stress the ambiguities of *infelix:* unfortunate for Pallas first, then for Turnus (and finally for Aeneas, Vergil seems to imply). Humphries calls the belt "of evil omen not only to Pallas now"; Lewis describes it as "a symbol of triumph and doom." The positions of *inimicum* and *saevi* also contribute to their ambiguity.[5]

As Aeneas seethes with fury and strikes the deadly blow, Vergil leaves little doubt that this is an act of violence more appropriate to Juno's creatures. The poet has, for example, earlier used the same phrase *furiis accensus* in 7.392 to characterize the irrational behavior of the Italian women excited by Amata; and the grotesque portrait of Turnus trying out his armor (12.101 ff.) employs the same imagery of furies, fire, anger, and frightfulness. Copley alone gives full stress to the metaphors: "A flame of fury and dreadful rage flared up." Humphries and Lewis both mute Vergil's tones, as if they cannot perceive or will not accept the grim pessimism of the *Aeneid*'s conclusion. Humphries omits the telling metaphors altogether and merely gives the phrase "terrible in wrath," and Lewis does much the same, while expanding Vergil's two words into two jerky sentences: "Rage shook him. He looked frightening." Their Aeneas is merely an indignant hero, not the wretched man whose act, Vergil expects us to see, borders on monstrous inhumanity.

The final important adjective, *fervidus* in 951, occupies a special position at the end of its sentence, after its verb, isolated by striking enjambment. Not one of our three translators can cope with its position; not one attempts to retain the metaphorical sense of "hot" despite the fact that the metaphor belongs to the image of fire already stated in *accensus*. Yet Vergil intends our last impression of Aeneas to be controlled by *fervidus,* and he stresses the point by isolating the word and placing it in the same line where he develops a contrasting picture of Turnus with alliterative *frigore*. While Aeneas is hot with destructive anger, Turnus lies cold in death at his feet.

One cannot fully appreciate the art of Vergilian epithets unless one knows that special position is determined not only by unusual order and wide separation from the noun but also by the way a word fits into the hexameter. Because each line is felt as a complete hexameter, Latin poets often ended their phrases or sentences with the line and placed a significant word in that final position. It would follow that after a full stop at the end of the previous line, the initial position of the next line would also be potentially emphatic. But when the poet varied this technique by running one line into the next, the initial position acquired major emphasis. We see this not only with *fervidus* in 951 but also with *terribilis* in 947. The same phenomenon, initial position after enjambment, accounts for the added force given *balteus* (942) and the names *Aeneas* and *Pallantis*—all three also pulled out of usual prose position—and the verbs *straverat* (944), *eripiare* (948), and *immolat* (949).

Vergil's emphatic use of adjectives, his artful positioning of key words, and his consistent treatment of thematic imagery are crucial aspects of his style and challenge every translator. On his sound and rhythmic patterns we might also make a few comments. Besides the alliteration of 951 which helps to stress the antithesis between *fervidus* and *frigore,* consider the potential pathos of *Pallantis pueri* in 943 ("Pallas, poor child") and *victum vulnere;* listen to the hissing sibilants of Aeneas' irrational rage in 949, *scelerato ex sanguine sumit.* Most of this is beyond translation. Vergil's mastery of hexameter rhythms evoked marvel in his own day; today we can hardly hope to duplicate it. I merely note the rhythmic art of the last three lines, which report the death of Turnus. In 950 Vergil uses the maximum number of spondees (two long syllables) to slow down the pace and fix our attention on the horror of killing. The first word of 951 is the isolated dactyl *fervidus;* it provides our last stark impression of Aeneas. Then as we turn away to look at Turnus, Vergil emphasizes the contrast with a set of three spondees: (*ast il li sōl vūntūr*) the limbs *slowly* relax in the cold grip of death. In 952 Turnus' life-force flees from his dead body in a rush of speedy dactyls (vītăqŭe cŭm gĕmĭ tū fŭgit); Vergil slows down only when he reaches *indignata* to stress the rage of the defeated soul. The basic iambic pentameter of Humphries and Copley cannot even attempt to capture such rhythmic effects, and Lewis, in his longer line, fails to come close:

> So saying, Aeneas angrily plunged his sword full into
> Turnus' breast. The body went limp and cold. With a deep sigh
> The unconsenting spirit fled to the shades below.

To describe all the stylistic techniques of Vergil would be an impossible task. Take for example the precisely chosen nonthematic metaphor *immolat* (949): Aeneas claims that the act of killing is really a "sacrifice"—only Humphries translates this—that through him as "high priest" Pallas exacts atonement for sin. That one ironic word epitomizes the horror of the scene. Notice how *vulnere Pallas* in 948 takes the same position in the line as *vulnere Turnus* in 943: one wound demands another. Then there are the repetitions in the last two lines. I have already indicated that *furiis accensus* (946) repeats a phrase from 7.392 and so likens Aeneas to a creature of Juno. The final line of Book Twelve, as is well known, repeats 11.831 and would remind a Roman of a formulaic line from the *Iliad*. Thus Turnus' death resembles not only the pathetic end of youthful Camilla but also the fateful death of Hector at Achilles' hands (*Iliad*, 22.362–63). With him perishes Italian resistance, just as Hector's fall meant the fall of Troy. In 951, Vergil also echoes an earlier passage, with irony that is not often remarked. The words *solvuntur frigore membra* exactly repeat the half-line from 1.92—the phrase appears nowhere else in the *Aeneid*—in which Vergil portrayed the chill *despair* of Aeneas as Juno's storm struck his fleet off Sicily. Aeneas, who claims that he is a priest sacrificing, in fact acts with the savage fury of Juno, and chill death spreads over the body of his victim Turnus. What a reversal from that earlier more innocent moment when Aeneas was Juno's victim, when he was chilled by her hot fury.

This particularization of Vergil's artistic techniques explains to a great extent both why translators fail with the *Aeneid* and why readers of Latin are endless admirers of the epic despite its inferiority as a "good story." Without the style of the original Latin, which cannot be adequately transmitted to another language, an essential part of the epic's meaning is lost. This "meaning" lies in details; it also lies in the whole poem. And before we leave the question, we should attempt to assess the effect of Vergilian style as a whole.

Vergil's artistic style is both artificial and sophisticated. Those adjectives, I suspect, account for the failure of the *Aeneid* in the Romantic and Victorian eras and for the dislike which many a schoolchild once felt toward him.[6] In the United States, where Latin in schools has declined, Vergil has benefited recently by gaining readers of college age and maturity. He did not write for schoolboys and girls, never intended his epic, on which he had labored ten years, to be the first major obstacle to young people's enjoyment of the Latin language and the Roman mind. In his day it was a fate worse than death to have one's priceless literary efforts fall into the hands of teachers and their restless pupils. For Vergil, the result of treating the *Aeneid* as a schoolbook has too often been that the teachers have struggled to teach the epic as an adventure story. They have had to choose the love affair with Dido as the greatest episode, and even there they have not been able to deal satisfactorily with the style or themes of the poem so as to explain why Dido is a comparative failure, Aeneas a comparative success. Teachers have not effectively conveyed and pupils under fifteen have not readily appreciated or responded to the sophisticated style upon which so much of the *Aeneid*'s meaning depends.

Now that college students read him—even in English translations—Vergil has begun to recover the reader he wrote for. Plot is minimal in the *Aeneid*. We could reduce the events of Book Twelve, for example, to the level of a TV western. Turnus, who has bravely led the opposition to Aeneas but resorted to unnecessary violence, has avoided direct confrontation with Aeneas. At last the inevitable combat takes place, and Aeneas kills Turnus. Hollywood's style would make a stirring technicolor "epic" from that plot. Vergil does not do so and accordingly foils the efforts of teachers looking for an adventure story; Vergil's style complicates the plot, mutes its potentially strident notes of heroism, and demands attention from the audience's intelligence as well as its emotions. I must insist that Vergil's original audience consisted of men who, like himself, were intelligent, practical, articulate, literate. They were people who had immersed themselves in politics and who had managed to survive the bitter years of Rome's civil wars. Now they welcomed the Augustan peace, but observed with considerable doubt and distrust the methods by which Augustus was restoring political order. For such men of the world it would be absurd to simplify life into black and white terms, as if Turnus were the villain, Aeneas the perfect hero. Relying on their political and literary sophistication, Vergil forged his complicated style as a vehicle for conveying his complex vision of Rome.

We have commented on the individual artistic devices of 12.938 ff. How does the passage work as a whole? I have argued, in the preceding chapter, that the effect is ambiguous. Not that Vergil has no convictions and is playing it safe as a smart court writer. Rather, he sees all sides of the issue and tries to present them for our judgment. Aeneas does not win a clear victory; Turnus does not deserve unreserved pity; the death is neither "butchery" nor "solemn sacrifice." Using the various techniques at his disposal as carefully and thoughtfully as he ever had, Vergil studied the death scene and accumulated around it a series of relevant impressions—some sympathetic to Aeneas, others conveying shocked disapproval—no single impression being allowed to prevail. We cannot cancel out the positive aspects of Aeneas' humane hesitation to kill or of his genuine grief for Pallas; nor can we ignore, as Humphries and Lewis tend to, the savage Aeneas who aligns himself paradoxically with the destructive purposes of Juno. Aeneas' father told him during the visit to the underworld that he should spare the conquered and war down the proud: *parcere subiectis et debellare superbos* (6.853). Yet here is a moment when the easy formula of Anchises is impossible to carry out faithfully. On the one hand, Turnus has been defeated and publicly confessed himself beaten: according to the formula he should be spared. On the other hand, he still sports arrogantly the spoils he stripped from Pallas in that duel which was really no duel but the slaughter of a boy by a man; Aeneas sees him exactly as he imagined him at the time of Pallas' death (*superbum caede nova,* 10.514–15): the formula justifies total extermination of such pride. We cannot fix on one detail or image alone and let that determine our interpretation of the *Aeneid's* close. Turnus' spirit has no clearer impression of the total situation, when it rages at the injustice it suffers (*indignata* 952), than Aeneas' fury has when he presents himself as a priest impersonally acting for Pallas to wipe out a sin. As Vergil has planned it, we must take in all these antitheses, half-truths, prejudiced emotions, metaphors, and see that Rome is permanently compromised. Not blackened or unblemished, but compromised. Each Roman had to adjust to that compromise as best he could.

Presenting an act so stark as the killing of Turnus in this sophisticated, unbiased manner, then ending the epic without further comment on Aeneas' mission has not succeeded with many audiences. Some have preferred to read into Vergil a simple thesis, ignoring the implications of his style. If, however, we overcome our own simplistic views, we can perhaps see that Vergil's perception is far more profoundly rooted in truth. When one great warrior, rejecting pleas for mercy, kills another, it is a human tragedy, and *infelix* is the appropriate word to introduce the fateful change of Aeneas' hesitation into savage use of the sword. But who are we, who is the poet to award neat labels of praise and blame? Does Turnus understand himself as he pleads for mercy any better than Aeneas as he kills? Vergil does not say. He asks for understanding of both men and what they represent for Rome and humanity. Moreover, by the very fact that he has reproduced this scene with such conviction through his artistic devices, he affords us some comfort: there is a poetic order, at least, where even the killing of a fellow human can be accepted and receive the artistic love that emerges in the patent craftsmanship of these final lines of the *Aeneid.*

CHRONOLOGY

B.C.

70	Vergil born near Mantua, October 5th.	Pompey and Crassus consuls.
63	Vergil living in Cremona.	Cicero consul; Catiline's conspiracy. Birth of C. Octavius (later Augustus).
60	Vergil studying in Cremona.	Formation of First Triumvirate: Caesar, Pompey, and Crassus.
59		Caesar consul.
58		Caesar begins Gallic campaign.
55		Pompey and Crassus consuls again.
54	Vergil completes school in Cremona; goes to Milan.	Crassus sets out for Parthia.
53	Vergil goes to Rome for legal training.	Crassus killed at Carrhae in Parthia.
52–50	Vergil gradually rejects other vocations, devotes self exclusively to poetry.	Tension between Pompey and Caesar moves Rome to brink of civil war.
49	Vergil probably living in Cumae in Epicurean society, writing.	Caesar crosses Rubicon, rapidly drives Pompey out of Italy.
44		Caesar murdered; by his will, C. Octavius adopted (hence Octavian).
42		Philippi: Brutus and Cassius defeated by Antony and Octavian.
41	Vergil begins *Eclogues*: I and IX deal with farmers facing confiscation.	Octavian confiscates much land around Cremona for his veterans.
39–		

B.C.

38	*Eclogues* completed; *Georgics* started.	Antony marries Octavia.
31	*Georgics* completed; *Aeneid* started.	Octavian defeats Antony and Cleopatra at Actium.
27		Octavian hailed as Augustus.
23	Reference to Marcellus in *Aenied*, 6.860 ff.	Marcellus, Augustus' nephew, dies.
19	Having completed most of *Aeneid*, Vergil sails to Greece to devote three years to revision. But Augustus persuades him to return to Italy. Sick on return trip, Vergil dies just after landing in Brindisi, September 21st.	Augustus travels in East to secure the empire, especially from the Parthians. On death of Vergil, publication of *Aeneid* entrusted to Vergil's friends, talented poets named Varius and Tucca.
17	Aeneid probably already published as part of Augustus' celebrations.	Secular games of Augustus; Horace commissioned to write special ode.

◆§ APPENDIX II §◆

FURTHER READING

W.A. Camps, *An Introduction to the Aeneid*. Oxford, 1969.

Wendell Clausen, *Virgil's Aeneid and the Tradition of Hellenistic Poetry*. Berkeley, Calif.: University of Calif. Press, 1987.

Steele Commager, ed., *Virgil, A Collection of Critical Essays*. Englewood Cliffs, N.J.: Prentice-Hall, Inc., 1966. Abbreviated in the notes as Commager, *Vergil*.

G.B. Conte, *The Rhetoric of Imitation. Genre and Poetic Memory in Virgil and other Latin Poets*. Ithaca, N.Y.: Cornell University Press, 1986.

G.K. Galinsky, *Aeneas, Sicily, and Rome*. Princeton, N.J.: Princeton University Press, 1969.

K.W. Gransden, *Virgil's Iliad: An Essay on Epic Narrative*. Cambridge: Cambridge University Press, 1984.

Gilbert Highet, *The Speeches in Vergil's Aeneid*. Princeton, N.J.: Princeton University Press, 1972.

W.R. Johnson, *Darkness Visible*. Berkeley, Calif.: University of Calif. Press, 1976.

G. Knauer, *Die Aeneis und Homer*. Goettingen, 1964.

M.O. Lee, *Fathers and Sons in Virgil's Aeneid*. SUNY Press, Albany, 1979.

R.O.A.M. Lyne, *Further Voices in Virgil's Aeneid*. Oxford, 1987.

Sara Mack, *Patterns of Time in Vergil*. Hamden, Conn., 1978.

Brooks Otis, *Virgil, A Study in Civilized Poetry*. New York: Oxford University Press, 1964. Abbreviated as Otis.

Victor Poeschl, *The Art of Vergil: Image and Symbol in the Aeneid,* trans. G. Seligson. Ann Arbor, Mich.: University of Michigan Press, 1962. Abbreviated as Poeschl, *The Art of Vergil*.

M. C. J. Putnam, *The Poetry of the Aeneid*. Cambridge: Cambridge University Press, 1965. Abbreviated as Putnam, *The Poetry of the Aeneid*.

Kenneth Quinn, *Virgil's Aeneid: a Critical Description*. Ann Arbor, Mich.: University of Michigan Press, 1968. Abbreviated as Quinn.

❧ NOTES ❧

Chapter I

[1] Varro of Atax wrote an *Argonautica* in the 30's or 20's. We hear of poets taking the exploits of Caesar in Gaul as their epic topic: for example, Furius Bibaculus.

[2] Lucan, by choosing the civil wars as his topic and also perceiving their relevance to the Neronian regime, lessened the distance between poet and matter. It was Dante, however, who broke the pattern when he inserted himself as the central character of his epic.

[3] On the *Eclogues*, see Otis, pp. 97 ff.; and V. Pöschl, *Die Hirtendichtung Virgils* (Heidelberg, 1964).

[4] On the *Georgics*, see Otis, pp. 144 ff.; and H. Altevogt, *Labor improbus. Eine Vergilstudie* (Münster, 1952).

[5] Basic to this subject and many others involving the *Aeneid* is R. Heinze, *Vergils epische Technik*, whose latest edition of 1915 was reprinted in 1957 at Darmstadt. For more recent works, see my studies, "Vergil's Second *Iliad*," *TAPA*, 88 (1957), 17–30, and "On Vergil's Use of the *Odyssey*," *Vergilius* (1963), pp. 1–8; also, R. D. Williams, "Vergil and the *Odyssey*," *Phoenix*, 17 (1963), 266–74; finally, G. N. Knauer, *Die Aeneis und Homer*, Hypomnemata VII (Göttingen, 1964). The portions of Otis' book which bear on the topic are printed by Commager in *Vergil*, pp. 89 ff.

[6] See Otis' chapter "The Subjective Style," pp. 41 ff.

[7] See Pöschl, *The Art of Vergil*, pp. 16 ff.; L. A. MacKay, "Saturnia Iuno," *Greece & Rome*, 3 (1956), 59–60, and my article, "Juno and Saturn in the *Aeneid*," *Studies in Philology*, 55 (1958), 519–32.

[8] On the *Odyssey*, see H. W. Clarke, *The Art of the Odyssey* in this Landmarks series (Englewood Cliffs, N.J.: Prentice-Hall Inc., 1967).

[9] See U. Knoche, "Zur Frage der epischen Beiwörter in Vergils Aeneis," *Festschrift Snell* (Hamburg, 1956), pp. 89–100; P. Grimal, "Pius Aeneas," Lecture to Vergil Society (London, 1959); W. R. Johnson, "Aeneas and the Ironies of Pietas," *CJ*, 60 (1965), 359–64.

Journals are abbreviated as follows: *AJP—American Journal of Philology; CJ—Classical Journal; CQ—Classical Quarterly; TAPA—Transactions of American Philological Association.*

Chapter II

[1] Pöschl, *Art of Vergil*, pp. 13 ff.; now available in Commager, *Vergil*, pp. 164 ff.

[2] See F. L. Newton, "Recurrent Imagery in *Aeneid* IV," *TAPA*, 88 (1957), 31–43.

[3] See G. E. Duckworth, "The Architecture of the *Aeneid*," *AJP*, 75 (1954), 1–15; "The *Aeneid* as a Trilogy," *TAPA*, 88 (1957), 1–10; and "Tripartite Structure in the *Aeneid*," *Vergilius*, 7 (1961), 2–11; also, W. A. Camp, "A Second Note on the Structure of the *Aeneid*," *CQ*, 9 (1959), 53–56.

[4] G. E. Duckworth, "Mathematical Symmetry in Vergil's *Aeneid*," *TAPA*, 91 (1960), 184–220; *Structural Patterns and Proportions in Vergil's Aeneid* (Ann Arbor, Mich.: University of Michigan Press, 1962).

[5] See B. M. W. Knox, "The Serpent and the Flame," *AJP*, 71 (1950), 379–400, reprinted in Commager, *Vergil*, pp. 124 ff.; and M. C. J. Putnam, *The Poetry of the Aeneid* (Cambridge, 1965), pp. 3 ff.

[6] See R. G. Austin, "Vergil, *Aeneid* II, 567–587," *CQ*, 11 (1961), 185–98.

[7] See Chapter One, pp. 21–22.

Chapter III

[1] For a similar analysis, see Otis, p. 253; and Quinn, p. 125. See also R. B. Lloyd, "*Aeneid* III, a New Approach," *AJP*, 78 (1957), 133–41. The importance of the central episode has been stressed by R. E. Grimm, "Aeneas and Andromache in *Aeneid* 3," *AJP*, 88 (1967), 151–62.

[2] It is plain that much time has passed when Aeneas arrives in Buthrotum (291 ff.), for Neoptolemos took Andromache as concubine, had a child by her, then was murdered by Orestes at Delphi, and his kingdom in Epirus has been radically changed by Andromache and Helenus (who seized power there). See also 5.626 for reference to seven years.

[3] The themes of exhaustion and weariness are well treated by A. W. Allen, "The Dullest Book of the *Aeneid*," *CJ*, 47 (1951), 119–23.

[4] See Pöschl; F. L. Newton, "Recurrent Imagery in *Aeneid* IV," *TAPA*, 88 (1957), 31–43; and B. Fenik, "Parallelism of Theme and Imagery in *Aeneid* II and IV," *AJP*, 80 (1959), 1–24.

[5] A. S. Pease, *Publi Vergili Maronis Aeneidos liber quartus* (Cambridge, 1935), has provoked many smiles by his sober refusal to exercise his imagination (p. 45): "Vergil intended, I believe, to leave in doubt the exact nature and extent of Aeneas's relations to Dido, and, whether we view the matter from the side of the legal evidence or from that of human charity, in doubt we may well leave it; *honi soit qui mal y pense.*"

[6] Euripides apparently considered it a stock motif: compare Admetus in *Alcestis*, 328 ff., and Theseus in *Hippolytos*, 860 ff.

[7] For a thorough analysis of Vergilian half-lines, see J. Sparrow, *Half-lines and Repetitions in Virgil* (Oxford, 1931).

[8] Vergil's use of the phrase *pius Aeneas* might be considered sardonic in 4.393,

but that, I believe, would be an act of "modern" cynical criticism, which has as little to do with Vergil's artistry as Victorian sentimentality once did. Vergil registers the problems besetting Aeneas' *pietas;* he never sneers at the attribute or intends us to.

Chapter IV

¹ See M. C. J. Putnam, "Unity and Design in *Aeneid* V," *Harvard Studies in Classical Philology,* 66 (1962), 205–39 (now reprinted in *The Poetry of the Aeneid,* pp. 64 ff.).

² Vergil's handling of Homer is well discussed in Heinze, pp. 145 ff.

³ Dido is specifically named in 571, but many of the prizes awarded by Aeneas may be derived from his stay in Carthage: for example, the Gaetulian lionskin (351), the Amazonian quiver (311), the horse (310), the purple chlamys (250).

⁴ In the chariot race of the *Iliad* Menelaus lost because of the underhand devices of Antilochus; Homer has no interest in the "moral explanation" of victory.

⁵ In Homer's footrace, a runner slips in a heap of dung, which has none of the aesthetic or symbolic value of this pool of blood.

⁶ Homer gives a brief report of a boxing match in which confident Epeios defeats with no difficulty his challenger Euryalus.

⁷ Homer limits the contest to two archers, Meriones and Teucer, who perform the actions of Mnestheus and Eurytion respectively in Vergil.

⁸ Vergil has certainly studied and occasionally echoes, especially in Book Four, Catullus' superb dramatization of Ariadne in Carmen 64. See D. E. Abel, "Aeneas and Dido," *Classical Bulletin,* 38 (1962), 57–61; G. Gonnelli, "Presenza di Catullo in Virgilio," *Giornale italiano di filologia,* 15 (1962), 225–53; P. Oksala, "Das Aufblühen des römischen Epos: Berührungen zwischen der Ariadne-Episode Catulls und der Dido-Geschichte Vergils," *Arctos,* 3 (1962), 167–97.

⁹ For other symbolic associations, see W. F. J. Knight, *Cumaean Gates* (Oxford, 1936).

¹⁰ See my article "Vergil's Second *Iliad,*" *TAPA,* 88 (1957), 17–30.

¹¹ See R. A. Brooks, "*Discolor aura.* Reflections of the Golden Bough," *AJP* 74 (1953), 260–80 (reprinted in Commager, *Vergil,* pp. 143 ff.).

¹² See B. Otis, "Three Problems of *Aeneid* 6," *TAPA,* 90 (1959), 165–79.

Chapter V

¹ Vergil seems to have made a mistake here or left the earlier passage unrevised, for Aeneas credits the prediction in 123 to Anchises.

² See K. J. Reckford, "Latent Tragedy in *Aeneid* VII, 1–285," *AJP,* 82 (1961), 252–69.

³ On Turnus' armor, see S. Small, "The Arms of Turnus, *Aeneid* VII, 783–792," *TAPA,* 90 (1959), 243–52. See also R. D. Williams, "The Function and Structure of Vergil's Catalogue in *Aeneid* VII," *CQ,* 11 (1961), 146–53.

⁴ On Book Eight, see Putnam, *The Poetry of the Aeneid,* pp. 105 ff.

[5] See my article on Propertius 4.9, *"Hercules exclusus,"* in *AJP*, 85 (1964), 1–12. For a comparison of the way Vergil and Ovid treated the subject, see B. Otis, *Ovid as an Epic Poet* (Cambridge, 1966), pp. 25 ff.

[6] The word Cacus seems to be an etymological play on the Greek word *kakos*, meaning "evil." See G. K. Galinsky, "The Hercules-Cacus Episode in *Aeneid* VIII," *AJP*, 87 (1966), 18–51.

Chapter VI

[1] Turnus, impaling the heads of Nisus and Euryalus on spears, resembles Cacus, who also exposed his victims' heads (8.196).

[2] See Otis, pp. 342 ff.

[3] Vergil uses the pathetic line ending *mortalibus aegris* elsewhere. In a contrasting situation, Aeneas tells how sleep came upon poor mortals the last night of Troy (2.268).

[4] In 10.276 Vergil has copied 9.126 almost exactly.

[5] Although Vergil does apostrophize Cydon as *infelix* (325), we do not feel that Aeneas is being criticized.

Chapter VII

[1] Compare *Iliad*, 6.506 ff. and 15.263 ff.

[2] It was apparently conventional, for example, to compare Drances to Cicero.

[3] The prototype for this debate is the mythical argument between Ajax the warrior and Odysseus the man of guile concerning the armor of Achilles.

[4] Vergil parallels a scene from *Iliad*, Book Six, in which Trojan women appeal vainly for Minerva's (Athena's) aid.

[5] See T. G. Rosenmeyer, "Vergil and Heroism: *Aeneid* XI," *CJ*, 55 (1960), 159–64.

[6] See Putnam, *Poetry of the Aeneid*, pp. 151 ff.; and Quinn pp. 252 ff.

[7] Vergil never interprets Lavinia's feelings toward Turnus or Aeneas. It is clearly possible to explain her blush in several fashions, indeed to attribute it to her affection for Amata alone. We see how Turnus is moved, but his wild emotions may completely misinterpret the situation.

[8] This bull simile and the earlier one of 103 ff. (applied to Turnus alone) both ultimately echo a single passage in *Georgics*, 3.219 ff. We cannot be sure how far the earlier passage controlled Vergil's imagination in *Aeneid*, Book Twelve, but it is at least tempting to believe that some ironic links exist. Turnus seems to play the role of the defeated bull in 103. What sets the bulls to fighting is passion over a cow, which Vergil in the *Georgics* treats as an animal instinct subject to intelligent control by the farmer. Should these two human bulls also be able to control their murderous fury—especially since they appear to battle for supremacy, not possession of a cow? With regard to *Daunius heros* in 723, I suggest that Vergil emphasizes *Daunius* more than *heros:* it becomes increasingly important to remember that Turnus' father Daunus anxiously awaits his son's return.

[9] In addition to portraying Turnus' irrationality, Vergil has succeeded in

avoiding a military impasse. To match a Vulcan-made sword against Vulcan-made armor would be tantamount to sending the theoretically irresistible missile against the impenetrable and indestructible surface!

[10] Vergil again explicitly alludes to *Iliad*, Book Twenty-two, where Homer referred to the "race" for the prize of Hector's life.

[11] In 928 *remugit* harkens back to 722.

[12] There are obvious aspects in which Aeneas' actions represent a "betrayal" of the ideal: first, he fails to chain up alive the human incarnation of *Furor impius* (compare 1.294); second, he fails to obey Anchises' lesson in "sparing the defeated" (compare 6.853).

[13] For other recent attempts, compare Otis, pp. 379 ff.; Putnam; Quinn, pp. 271 ff.; and R. Beare, "Invidious Success. Some Thoughts on the End of the *Aeneid*," *Proceedings of the Vergilian Society*, 4 (1964), 18–30.

Chapter VIII

[1] Some of the problems of translation are well analyzed by R. W. B. Lewis, "On Translating the Aeneid: Yif that I Can," *Yearbook of Comparative and General Literature*, 10 (1961), 7–15 (reprinted in Commager, *Vergil*, pp. 41 ff.).

[2] Note that in this passage the only adjective to follow its noun, *alto* in 941, is separated from it so as to occupy the important final position of the line and to form with *umero* a rhetorical phrase that effectively surrounds the verb.

[3] On Vergilian practice with adjectives, see F. J. Wortsbrock, *Elemente einer Poetik der Aeneis* (Münster, 1963). For personal epithets, a useful work is that of N. Mosely, *Characters and Epithets: a Study in Vergil's Aeneid* (New Haven: Yale University Press, 1926).

[4] I shall be using as representative translators in this chapter three men whose work is modern and whose aim is to be as faithful as possible to the poetic form: R. Humphries, *The Aeneid of Virgil: A Verse Translation* (New York and London: Charles Scribner's Sons, 1954); C. D. Lewis, *The Aeneid of Virgil: A New Verse Translation* (New York: Doubleday Anchor, 1953); and F. O. Copley, *Vergil: The Aeneid* (Indianapolis: Bobbs-Merrill, 1965).

[5] The ambiguity of *inimicum* consists in the fact that it could refer to the enemy Pallas, whose belt Turnus stripped away, or to Turnus rendered hateful to Aeneas by what he had so arrogantly done to Pallas. In *saevi*, too, there is ambiguity: it might stress the heavy blow to Aeneas' affectionate relationship with Pallas or the savage anger which Turnus aroused.

[6] For a typical misinterpretation of Vergil based on boyhood prejudices, see Robert Graves, "The Virgil Cult," *Virginia Quarterly Review*, 38 (Winter, 1962), 13–35.

INDEX

A

Achilles, 5, 6, 20, 56, 57, 90
Achilles like Aeneas, 51, 73, 82
Actium, 11, 18, 63, 72, 73
Aeneas (*see also* Achilles, Hercules, Odysseus):
  armor, 70, 72, 97
  and Augustus, 11, 18, 19, 81
  commission, 34, 37
  and history, 16, 17
  as leader, 12, 16, 41, 50
  in love, 43, 44, 46, 48, 59, 67
  and Paris, 57, 66
  passionate, 33, 35, 84, 98, 99
  passive, 14, 15, 16, 100
  personal satisfaction, 15
  pius, 21, 22, 47, 54, 67, 84, 85, 93, 94, 100, 103
  rationality, 46
  responsibility, 45
  transformed, 83, 103
  victims of, 26, 47, 82, 84, 99
  warrior, 15, 71, 82, 97
Aeneid:
  beginning, 2, 5
  editing, 5, 36
  publication, 5
Aeolus, 13, 24
Alba Longa, 16, 17
Allecto, 13, 66 ff.
Amata, 67, 93, 96
Ambivalence, 26, 104
Anchises, 36, 38, 40, 54, 60, 108
Andromache, 39, 41, 42
Antony, 4
Apollo, 40, 56, 64

Apollonius, 45

Ariadne, 56
Ascanius, 17, 27, 54, 68, 79
Athena, 20
Augustine, 14
Augustus, 5, 11, 25, 61, 63, 69, 71, 72, 73; *see also* Aeneas, Octavian
Autobiography, 2

B

Banquet, 29, 30
Brutalization, 8, 9
Burning ships, 54, 76
Buthrotum, 39

C

Cacus, 71, 97
Caesar, 1, 4
Calypso, 7, 42
Camilla, 70, 90, 91
Carthage, 13, 22, 27, 31, 49, 65
Circe, 7
Civil war, *see* War
Comic, 53
Conventions, epic: 2, 3, 5
  divine machinery, 19 ff.
  impersonality, 3, 6, 9
  objectivity, 3
Council of gods, 80, 81
Crete, 40
Creusa, 22, 37, 40, 67
Critics: Romantic, Victorian, 45, 47, 107
Cumae, 15, 18, 50, 55
Cupid, 29
Cybele, 77